The Written Word   Book 1

The Written Word Book 1

A Course in Controlled Composition

Tom McArthur

Oxford University Press

Oxford University Press
Walton Street, Oxford OX2 6DP

Oxford New York
Athens Auckland Bangkok Bombay
Calcutta Cape Town Dar es Salaam Delhi
Florence Hong Kong Istanbul Karachi
Kuala Lumpur Madras Madrid Melbourne
Mexico City Nairobi Paris Singapore
Taipei Tokyo Toronto

and associated companies in
Berlin Ibadan

OXFORD and OXFORD ENGLISH are trade marks
of Oxford University Press

ISBN 0 19 451360 2

First published 1984
Ninth impression 1995

No unauthorized photocopying

The publishers would like to thank the following for
permission to reproduce photographs.

John Cleare/Mountain Camera
Donald Cooper
Professor H. E. Edgerton
The Mary Evans Picture Library
Fay Goodwin
O. Winston Link
The Mansell Collection
Rosie Potter

Illustration on page 42 by Paul Wright
Cover illustration by Peter Till

Phototypeset in Linotron Sabon by
Tradespools Ltd, Frome, Somerset
Printed in Hong Kong

Acknowledgements

Firstly, Basil Skinner, Head of the Department of Extra-Mural Studies at the University of Edinburgh, Bridget Stevens, his Administrative Assistant, and William McDowall, Head of the Language Learning Centre. Without their help, when I was responsible for the Department's service courses in English as a foreign language, this course would never have come into existence. Additionally, the hard work and interest of many students of diverse linguistic and professional backgrounds taking the weekly courses between 1975 and 1979 were also invaluable in helping me see where I wanted to go. The present course owes much to them.

Secondly, Patricia Foy, Lorraine Therrien-Roy, and Claude Girard, three English language advisers in Quebec City, who made it possible for me to work, between 1979 and 1981, with twenty-two secondary school teachers, all of whom I would like to thank for their interest and inspiration.

Thirdly, colleagues at the Université du Quebec à Trois-Rivières: Ton That Thien for his comments, and Judith Cowan, Patricia Gordon and Gisèle Wilson, for using much of the material in their classes and providing useful feedback from all concerned. Additionally, my research students Lise Lachapelle, Susan MacNeil and André Rouleau, three insightful undergraduate students France Jutras, Cheryl Kosaka and Joane Turcotte, and many others who made useful observations on the material when we worked with it together.

Fourthly, Keith Doyle at Three Rivers High School, for assessing the material in relation to native and near native secondary school students of English.

Fifthly, those who have worked with Oxford University Press in helping me prepare the material for wider dissemination, particularly Henry Widdowson, Professor of Education (with special reference to speakers of other languages) University of London Institute of Education, and those within Oxford University Press for seeing me safely through the editorial and production stages of what remains one of the most enjoyable – if at times frustrating – projects I have ever worked on.

Lastly, my daughter Roshan, now fifteen, for her patient and good-humoured services as guinea-pig, demonstrating that the material has been comprehensible and I hope useful to at least one young native user of the language. For her help, many thanks.

Contents

Unit 4

Unit 5   Revision

Unit 6

Unit 7

To the teacher or administrator

The Written Word is the product of some eight years of experimentation and practical use, first at the University of Edinburgh and later at the University of Quebec.

In Edinburgh, the course originally developed as a means of helping foreign postgraduate students – working in subjects as diverse as architecture, geology, law, medicine, language teaching and the physical sciences – to write clearly and logically in English. In Quebec, it has been adapted to cover late secondary, junior college and university work. These two very distinct areas of work proved compatible largely because the basic skills of writing are the same for most people and most purposes. Everybody has to be able to write clearly, spell adequately, punctuate consistently, follow the rules of grammar, handle stylistic differences and, importantly, be aware of the options offered within what people see as 'good written English'. This is as true today as it was a hundred years ago.

The course is, however, 'controlled'. It does not encourage the student, in the early stages, to attempt a lot of free expression. In the writer's experience over twenty years of teaching English at various levels in various parts of the world, too much freedom in writing can mean frustration. One does not say to a new learner driver: 'Get into the car and start. Anywhere will do.' In the same way, pre-analysis of the problems together with guidance throughout the work itself are prerequisites for a student's success. The discipline is often welcomed with relief.

Under guidance of the kind provided here, the student can proceed at his or her own speed, benefiting from the chance to work privately – and writing is a private art – as well as, one hopes, the opportunity to consult a tutor regularly. Additionally, the format of the units, with their detailed answer sections, enables a tutor to look after anything from one to thirty students simultaneously, without getting flooded out with material to correct. Traditional writing courses can be very hard on the tutor. This one is not.

At the same time, no limitation is placed on any teacher who wishes to supplement the graded and guided material with related free composition. This is entirely a matter between teacher and student. The important thing is that the course provides a useful framework within and around which related work can be organized.

The principle animating the course is relatively simple: to give students clearcut quantities of interrelated material through which to proceed to higher levels of skill. Intermediate and even advanced foreign users of English can benefit from the layout, the instructions and the exercises, and in one compact system are provided with core information on grammar, levels of formality, spelling, punctuation, word use and formation, composition and editing. Having taught English as a mother tongue as well as a foreign or second language, I also suspect that the course – or courses like it – will serve native users of English too.

The techniques employed combine both 'traditional' and 'modern' methodology. Texts, lists, tables, analytical and synthetic procedures, blank-filling, multiple choice, conversion exercises, pattern practice, elements of programmed learning and even the correction of deliberate mistakes all rub shoulders amicably enough. Additionally, many of the students who took the original course in Edinburgh also used it as a preparation for the Cambridge Certificate examinations, with good results. Indeed, resemblances will be found between certain procedures here and in those examinations.

Not everything in the exercises has been explained in the instructions, partly because such a procedure would have made the course too bulky, and partly because it is natural and desirable that students should induce as much as possible by themselves. Since creative expression is very much a personal thing, however, it has been assumed that teachers can encourage the free development of writing skills, and also that a professional person can divert what he or she has learnt into the channels of special interest without further help from us.

Every effort has been made to avoid an unnatural or laboured style. Consequently, grammatical and other material often appears in the model texts before it is described and practised in the exercise sections. Thus, for example, quotation and parenthesis are both used freely before the student is asked to handle them. This, it is believed, is closer to real life than a strict gradation of material so that nothing is encountered until it can be explained.

To the student

1   This course is intended for people who have reached a reasonable level in reading and understanding the English language, the kind of level usually called 'intermediate'. Such people may or may not speak English well, but their ability to read will be much greater than their ability to write. (In practice, we have found that many 'advanced' students have benefited from doing systematic work of this kind. This includes many professional people capable of excellent written work in their own languages.)

2   The course is based on the assumption that writing well in any language is a difficult art and needs a great deal of practice. Writing adequately in a second language is often a slow, painful and frustrating experience.

3   The aim here is to make writing practice in English a pleasant, realistic and rewarding experience (at least as far as that is possible within the limits of a course of this kind). It will, however, necessitate hard work on your part.

4   The work should be done systematically. Do not, for example, start in the middle of Unit 2 because the earlier material seems too easy. It is not. It is also not a good idea to jump sections, because the units and sections are all carefully interrelated in order to provide you with the necessary repetitive practice as well as new experience.

5   If you feel at any time that the information or the answers are not in any way satisfactory, do not hesitate about consulting other sources or discussing the point in question with your tutor or a competent friend or colleague. Writing in English is an art, not part of a fixed science.

6   The language of the texts, instructions and exercises has been kept as simple as possible (especially in the earlier units), but where a choice was necessary between being simple and being natural, naturalness always won. If, consequently, you do not understand anything, consult a good dictionary (unilingual or bilingual) or grammar book. In a course of this length it is impossible (and undesirable) to try to explain everything.

7　　Resist the temptation to look at the answers until you have tried an exercise at least once. Additionally, even after seeing the answers once, be prepared to do an exercise again – and again, until you achieve a satisfactory level of performance. In writing, once is almost never enough. Do rough work where necessary, before making a final version of a piece of writing. (After doing the basic material, you may also wish to 'play' with the topic, developing it in your own way. Feel free to do so.)

8　　Do not accept from yourself a lower level of performance than you would accept from others:
* Is your handwriting as clear as it might be?
* Are you as careful about spelling and punctuation as you should be?
* Is grammar something you want to be reasonably exact about?
* If you type, do you take care with the organization of your page?

9　　Writing must be clear and logical – and simple writing is where one begins. Complexity is often necessary, when ideas are complex, but there is no advantage in complexity when the ideas are – *or should be* – simple.

10　　The basic principles of good writing are the same for all kinds of writing: story-telling, newspapers, business and scientific reports, material written for children or for adults, for general reading or for specialist purposes. This is a course in basic principles.

UNIT 1

1.1 Comprehension and composition model: 'Cats'

The original cast of the musical 'Cats' at the New London Theatre.

Here is a short passage about cats. It is presented as one complete paragraph. Read it twice.

Cats are independent animals. They are domestic animals, like dogs, but they are not so completely domestic as dogs. They like to keep some secrets. They have their own private lives. The domestic cat is very much a hunter and a wanderer like her bigger sisters, the lion and the tiger. The ancient Egyptians were probably the first 5 people to keep cats, but they did not keep them as pets. The cat was a god in ancient Egypt, or, more correctly, a goddess. It is an interesting fact that in English people usually refer to cats as female. A male cat gets a special name to show that he is not female. He is a 'tomcat'. In the English language, a woman is called a 'cat' if she 10 says unkind things about other women, but we do not call a man a 'cat' if he says unkind things about other men. If a man is not very nice, we call him a 'dog' or a 'rat'.

Below are some statements relating to the passage. Some of these statements are true (T) in terms of the passage, while others are false (F). Mark them appropriately, and if a statement is false, say why.

a. ☐ Cats are just as domestic as dogs.

b. ☐ Dogs like to keep some secrets.

c. ☐ Cats and lions are like each other in some ways.

d. ☐ The ancient Egyptians kept cats as pets.

e. ☐ People generally refer to a cat as 'she'.

f. ☐ A male cat is called a 'tomcat'.

g. ☐ A woman is called a 'cat' if she speaks unkindly about other people.

h. ☐ Men who are not very nice are sometimes called 'dogs' and 'rats', but never 'cats'.

1.2 Spelling: Doubling consonants

Look at these two pieces from the passage on cats:

1 . . . a *wanderer* like her *bigger* sisters, the   (lines *4–5*)
lion and the tiger.

2 . . . a god in ancient Egypt, or, more   (line *7*)
correctly, a *goddess*.

The *italicised* words in both pieces follow certain English spelling rules. These rules concern when to double (or *not* to double) certain consonants. Below is a list of words. Suffixes (like *-ed*, *-er*, *-est* and *-ing*) can be added to these words. Mark the words which must double their final consonants, and add at least one example of this happening. (The rules for doubling consonants are given in the answer section for this unit, in case you need to study them.)

a. kind   d. reckon
b. swim   e. plan
c. come   f. fat

g.	name	l.	determine
h.	develop	m.	nod
i.	quiet	n.	prefer
j.	occur	o.	gossip
k.	level	p.	permit

1.3 Grammar and structure: Tenses

The table below analyses how verbs are used in the passage. All the finite verbs (that is, all the verbs with subjects) are underlined, and the notes at the side refer to the tenses used.

simple present tense used for general statements	Cats are independent animals. They are domestic animals, like dogs, but they are not so completely domestic as dogs. They like to keep some secrets. They have their own private lives. The domestic cat is very much a hunter and a wanderer like her bigger sisters, the lion and the tiger.
simple past tense used for particular (historical) statements	The ancient Egyptians were probably the first people to keep cats, but they did not keep them as pets. The cat was a god in ancient Egypt, or, more correctly, a goddess.
return to the present tense for further general statements	It is an interesting fact that in English people usually refer to cats as female. A male cat gets a special name to show that he is not female. He is a 'tomcat'. In the English language, a woman is called a 'cat' if she says unkind things about other women, but we do not call a man a 'cat' if he says unkind things about other men. If a man is not very nice, we call him a 'dog' or a 'rat'.

In the passage, the general statements relate to things that still exist or happen, while the particular statements are about things that no longer exist or happen. This is just one pattern among many possible patterns where the present tense contrasts with the past. In the passages which occur later in this course you should make a habit of studying how the tenses are used. Suppose you changed everything in this passage into the past. What effect would this have?

1.4 Grammar and composition: Making connections

Below you will find two examples, some instructions and advice, and then two lists in a box. Follow the examples and turn the sentences into a paragraph about cats and dogs.

Example 1   Cats are domestic animals.   **but**
             They are not as domestic as dogs.

▷   Cats are domestic animals, but
     they are not as domestic as dogs.

Example 2   Dogs generally like to be part of the family.   **while**
             Cats like to keep some secrets of their own.

▷   Dogs generally like to be part of the family while
     cats like to keep some secrets of their own.

Using *but* and *while* you can contrast and compare various things. *But* makes a contrast very clear. *While* is not so strong, and simply makes a comparison. Now proceed with the following material. Write it out as a complete paragraph, using *but* and *while*.

First statements	Conjunctions	Second statements
Cats are independent animals.	**but**	Dogs are not.
Dogs generally like company.	**while**	Cats often prefer to keep to themselves.
Domestic cats still have a lot in common with their bigger sisters, the lion and the tiger.	**but**	Most domestic dogs do not have much in common with their wild relative, the wolf.
In ancient times, the cat was a goddess.	**while**	The dog was a worker, protecting the sheep and the home.
It is also interesting that in English the cat is female.	**but**	The dog is not, being generally regarded as male.
A male cat gets the special name 'tomcat' to show that he is not female.	**while**	The female dog gets the special name 'bitch' to show she is not male.

1.5 Punctuation:
The sentence and the period

The period or full-stop ends a sentence.↙

Sometimes, however, people forget to use it. Sometimes, they also put commas (,) between their sentences, instead of periods. This is probably because they do not see their sentences as complete pieces of information with independent grammatical forms. Such pieces of information need to be clearly separated from each other. The English language also uses capital letters at the beginning of sentences to make this separation even clearer, and therefore has a special way of marking both the start and the finish of a sentence.

The material in the boxes below is organized in order to show how important clear punctuation is. In the first box there is no punctuation at all, while underneath the same passage is adequately punctuated.

no periods, capital letters or commas	cats are independent animals they are domestic animals like dogs but they are not so completely domestic as dogs they like to keep some secrets they have their own private lives the domestic cat is very much a hunter and a wanderer like her bigger sisters the lion and the tiger
all the necessary marks	Cats are independent animals. They are domestic animals, like dogs, but they are not so completely domestic as dogs. They like to keep some secrets. They have their own private lives. The domestic cat is very much a hunter and a wanderer like her bigger sisters, the lion and the tiger.

In the second box, it is easier to see and to understand the separate pieces of information. We see clearly what the writer wants us to see, and may even manage to say it better.

Punctuation work:
First stage

If a passage is read aloud, the reader usually pauses at each period. The period in fact marks this spoken pause. A reader may also pause, briefly, at a comma, but may not, while the end of a paragraph often requires a longer pause than the end of a sentence.

Go back to the passage on cats at the beginning of this unit. Consider how you would read it aloud. Think about the pauses, but also think about how to stress the important words in the passage. Punctuation is closely related to speech, and learning how to read aloud properly is a great aid to good writing. In the answer section for this unit you will find the passage written out in a special way that may help you in reading aloud.

Punctuation work:
Second stage

Below is part of the passage on cats. It has no periods or capital letters at all, but it has some commas. Do not change any of the commas, but re-write the passage in full, properly punctuated.

the ancient egyptians were probably the first people to keep cats, but they did not keep them as pets the cat was a god in ancient egypt, or, more correctly, a goddess it is an interesting fact that people usually refer to cats as female a male cat gets a special name to show that he is not female he is a 'tomcat' in the english language, a woman is called a 'cat' if she says unkind things about other women, but we do not call a man a 'cat' if he says unkind things about other men if a man is not very nice, we call him a 'dog' or a 'rat'

Now do the same for this completely new passage:

a friend of mine has a cat called cleopatra this cat sometimes goes away for weeks, and no one sees her or knows where she is occasionally, however, my friend finds her sitting on a wall in the moonlight, miles from home cleopatra comes down from the wall, rubs herself against my friend to say 'hullo', then walks away again she comes back about a week later, quite happy, in her own good time cleopatra is independent she certainly lives with my friend, but she does not in any sense belong to him

1.6 Vocabulary: Forming words

Many useful words can be formed by adding suffixes to other words. Study the list and the example below, then complete the exercise.

1	a person or animal that *hunts*	a *hunter*
2	like a *cat*	*catlike/cat-like*
3	a female *god*	a *goddess*
4	causing *interest*	*interesting*
5	showing *interest*	*interested*

Example The cat is a _____ .   **hunt**

▷ The cat is a hunter.

a. Cats, lions and tigers are all _____ .   **wander**

b. Monkeys are _____ animals.   **man**

c. Which of those ladies was the _____ at the party?   **host**

d. _____ countries are not necessarily less interesting than industrial countries.   **develop**

e. He has studied at several universities and is a very _____ man.   **learn**

f. When the police found the dead body they began to look for the _____ .   **murder**

g. He was determined to finish the work; he worked on with _____ determination.   **dog**

h. He thinks a lot and is a good _____ .   **plan**

i. The mouse is a small _____ animal.   **rat**

j. She works very well; she is a very _____ _____ indeed.   **skill; work**

1.7 Grammar:
Articles, singulars and plurals

The following table contains several sentences from the passage on *Cats*:

Plurals only	Singulars with *the*
1 *Cats* are independent animals. They are domestic animals, like *dogs*, but they are not so completely domestic as *dogs*.	
	2 *The domestic cat* is very much a hunter and a wanderer like her bigger sisters, *the lion* and *the tiger*.
3 The ancient Egyptians were probably the first people to keep *cats*, but they did not keep them as pets.	
	4 *The cat* was a god in ancient Egypt, or, more correctly, a goddess.

Note   *The* is used with *Egyptians* because the definite article is regularly used with nationalities: *the Americans*, *the French*, etc.

In the sentences shown in this table the same animal is sometimes described in the singular with a definite article (*the cat*), sometimes in the plural without an article (*cats*). The meaning is essentially the same in both cases. When a writer thinks of an animal as a type (or, scientifically, as a *species*), then the form is *the cat*, *the dog*, etc. When the writer thinks of animals as many individuals, then the form is *cats*, *dogs*, etc. The same rule also applies to plants and to certain objects that can be classified into types.

Composition work:
First stage

Study the examples, then change the sentences in the same way.

Example 1	Cats are independent animals.	**emphasis on individuals**
▷	The cat is an independent animal.	**emphasis on the type**

a. Dogs generally like company.

b. Lions must kill in order to live.

c. Tigers are powerful animals.

d. Roses are beautiful flowers.

e. In ancient Egypt, cats were goddesses.

f. Squares are geometrical figures.

g. Trees are important in our lives.

h. Elephants are very large animals.

Example 2   The cat is an independent animal.

▷   Cats are independent animals.

i. He has been studying the tiger and its habits.

j. It is easier to grow the rose in some climates than in others.

k. The kangaroo is found in Australia, but the jaguar is native to Central and South America.

l. The cat was certainly considered divine in ancient Egypt.

m. The wolf and the hyena are wild animals, while the dog is a domestic animal.

n. The tiger and the lion are very large, but the domestic cat is relatively small.

o. Although some people prefer the rose, I prefer the tulip and the daffodil because they are spring flowers.

p. The circle and the triangle are both common figures in geometry.

In the above sentences, you simply followed the examples. Now study the following sentences carefully and decide how they could be changed from singular to plural, or plural to singular.

q. Oaks and elms are trees which grow slowly.

r. The rat is an animal that carries disease.

s. The dog is often called man's best friend.

t. Many people regard the oak tree as a symbol of strength.

u. Dogs are popular animals in English-speaking countries, but men are still called 'dogs' if they are not nice to people.

v. The ancient Greeks did not have a high opinion of the dog.

w. Deer are not usually domestic animals.

x. The sheep and the goat are similar, but they are not members of the same species.

Composition work:
Second stage

Below there are two paragraphs, each containing numbered blanks. Consider whether a definite article, an indefinite article or nothing at all is needed in those blanks. Insert the proper word or an 'X', as appropriate.

y. (1)_____ cats are independent animals. They are (2)_____ domestic animals, like (3)_____ dogs, but they are not so completely domestic as (4)_____ dogs. They like to keep some secrets. They have their own private lives. (5)_____ domestic cat is very much (6)_____ hunter and (7)_____ wanderer like her bigger sisters, (8)_____ lion and (9)_____ tiger.

z. (1)_____ cat is (2)_____ independent animal. It is (3)_____ domestic animal, like (4)_____ dog, but is not so completely domestic as (5)_____ dog. It likes to keep some secrets. It has its own private life. (6)_____ domestic cats are very much (7)_____ hunters and (8)_____ wanderers like their bigger sisters, (9)_____ lion and (10)_____ tiger.

1.8 Controlled composition:
Animal names

In the lists immediately below you will find the first three sentences of the passage on cats reduced to their essential content. They are now a little like a telegram. To return the sentences to their original form it is necessary to add the basic grammatical materials of English:

1 cat/be/independent/animal
2 they/be/domestic/animal/like/dog/but/be/not/so/complete/ domestic/as/dog
3 they/like/keep/some/secret

The verbs in the lists are underlined so that you will know that they *are* verbs and are not any other part of speech, and this practice will be followed in all the exercises like this throughout the course.

Below you will find two similar sets of lists. These serve as the basis for two passages about how we use the names of animals in everyday

English. Study the lists, then write the two paragraphs, taking care with spelling, punctuation, tenses, singulars and plurals, margins and general layout.

Animal names

1 in/English/language/name/of/animal/<u>be</u>/often/<u>use</u>/<u>describe</u>/ people

2 if/man/<u>be</u>/not/very/nice/some/people/<u>might</u>/<u>call</u>/he/'rat'

3 if/he/<u>be</u>/quiet/dull/and/not/very/brave/they/<u>might</u>/<u>call</u>/he/ 'mouse'

4 if/he/<u>try</u>/trick/other/people/they/<u>might</u>/<u>call</u>/he/'fox'

5 we/<u>do</u>/this/because/we/<u>think</u>/that/some/kind/of/animal/and/ some/kind/of/people/<u>share</u>/same/quality

1 in/English/we/sometimes/<u>use</u>/adjective/<u>take</u>/from/name/ animal/<u>describe</u>/other/thing

2 we/<u>say</u>/for/example/that/something/<u>be</u>/'fishy'/if/we/<u>feel</u>/that/it/ <u>have</u>/bad/smell/or/<u>be</u>/suspicious/in/some/way

3 we/sometimes/<u>say</u>/that/woman/<u>be</u>/'catty'/if/she/ <u>say</u>/unkind/thing/about/other/woman

4 people/<u>be</u>/'foxy'/if/they/<u>be</u>/always/<u>try</u>/trick/other/people

5 description/that/<u>use</u>/animal/name/<u>be</u>/usual/not/compliment

1.9 Controlled composition: Writing paragraphs

A paragraph consists of one or more sentences. It is generally all that a writer wants to say on a particular topic or part of a topic. Usually a paragraph begins with a *key* (or *topic*) *sentence*, which serves to open the paragraph and is followed by one or more other sentences that develop the topic. For example, the paragraph on cats has an organization as follows:

Plan	Contents of paragraph
1 key sentence	Cats are independent animals.
2 the cat's nature	They are ... the lion and the tiger
3 the cat in ancient Egypt	The ancient Egyptians ... a goddess.
4 cats being 'female'	It is an interesting fact ... a 'tomcat'.
5 uses of the word 'cat'	In the English language ... or a 'rat'.

Sometimes, for short reports or descriptions, one paragraph is enough. Usually, however, a piece of writing looks better (and is perhaps easier to read) if it is organized in more than one paragraph. When planning his or her work, a writer considers these points:

1   How many paragraphs are necessary? The writer plans to have a paragraph for each distinct topic or part of his main topic.

2   Whether to divide a longer paragraph into some shorter ones, in order to emphasize certain points or make the material easier to read.

3   The size of the page, the kind of writing or typeface, the size of the margins, etc, so that the paragraphs look attractive to the reader.

4   The age, ability and interests of the readers. Paragraphs in academic books generally look very different from paragraphs in children's books, and a specialist newspaper can look very different indeed from a newspaper for the general public.

The paragraph at the beginning of this unit is in the style of the general textbook, report or specialist magazine. Below, the same material is organized quite differently. This time it has one paragraph for each of the points in the plan. Here, the key sentence becomes the *key paragraph*.

Cats are independent animals.

They are domestic animals, like dogs, but they are not so completely domestic as dogs. They like to keep some secrets. They have their own private lives. The domestic cat is very much a hunter and a wanderer like her bigger sisters, the lion and the tiger.

The ancient Egyptians were probably the first people to keep cats, but they did not keep them as pets. The cat was a god in ancient Egypt, or, more correctly, a goddess.

It is an interesting fact that in English people usually refer to cats as female. A male cat gets a special name to show that he is not female. He is a 'tomcat'.

In the English language, a woman is called a 'cat' if she says unkind things about other women, but we do not call a man a 'cat' if he says unkind things about other men. If a man is not very nice, we call him a 'dog' or a 'rat'.

Notice also the special large margins used here to help demonstrate the way in which the material is presented. This is known technically as 'white space', and is an important factor in the attractive presentation of any written or printed page. A good writer, typist and publisher not only tries to write well, but is also very interested in how his or her work looks to the reader's eye.

Writing practice

Here is a plan for a short composition about people's attitudes towards animals around the world. It may be presented in one or more paragraphs, as you prefer. Each section of the plan contains one or more lists of basic words that must be combined grammatically. No additional information should be added.

1	key sentence/paragraph	People's attitudes to animals can be very different in different parts of the world.
2	an example of different attitudes	in/some/place/for/example/dog/be/popular/as/domestic/pet/but/in/other/they/be/never/<u>allow</u>/inside/house
		they/be/<u>keep</u>/outside/<u>help</u>/with/sheep/or/<u>guard</u>/property
3	a contrast: the cow in India and in the western world	in/India/cow/be/sacred/animal/and/be/never/<u>kill</u>/or/eat/while/in/western/world/cattle/<u>be</u>/<u>keep</u>/<u>provide</u>/milk/meat/and/people/<u>have</u>/no/special/feeling/about/they
4	attitudes to animals and our use of language	in/many/language/name/for/animal/be/<u>use</u>/<u>describe</u>/people
		this/name/<u>serve</u>/<u>express</u>/our/strong/opinion/<u>about</u>/both/animal/and/human/being/and/general/they/be/not/complimentary
		nobody/usual/<u>enjoy</u>/<u>be</u>/<u>compare</u>/animal
		in/modern/English/no/woman/<u>want</u>/be/compare/cat/or/cow/and/no/man/<u>want</u>/<u>be</u>/<u>call</u>/'dog'/or/'rat'
5	conclusion	from/point/view/science/like/zoology/of/course/this/comparison/<u>have</u>/no/meaning
		they/<u>relate</u>/instead/to/cultural/and/emotional/attitude/and/therefore/<u>interest</u>/people/who/study/human/mind

---

Before checking your work in the answer section, look over it again (with the help of a friend, if possible) and complete the following checklist:

Points	Yes	No
1 all the periods properly placed		
2 all the capital letters clearly written		
3 the margins sufficient and *straight*		
4 all the words properly spelled		
5 the 's' added as needed to all the plural nouns and singular verbs		
6 all the definite and indefinite articles in your opinion properly added		

1.10 Editing a text: Doing your own corrections

Every writer has to learn to check written work. Using what you have learned in this unit (and in any other course), study the following passage about horses and cows, correcting it as necessary:

Horses are useful animals, but they are not more usefull than cow. It is easier to ride horse than cow, but it is easier to milk a cow than horse. Cows are generally regarded as female, and the male get the special name 'bull' to show that he is not female. Horses, however, are generally regarded male, the female getting the special name mare to show that she is not male. We can, however, call male horse 'Stallion', but there is no special name, in english language at least. for female cow.

UNIT 2

2.1 Comprehension and composition model: 'The Journey'

Looking down on the town of Todmorden in Yorkshire, England.

Here is a short story about a journey. Note how it is laid out on the page, and then read it twice.

In those days, the journey from our village in the hills to the nearest big town was not an easy one. There was a bus twice a week, and it was necessary to walk about three kilometres to where the bus waited. There was no motor road to the village itself in those days. Nowadays, the villagers have a much easier life, and that long walk is unnecessary. 5

My father used to take things to sell in the town, and we carried everything down the steep, rocky path early in the morning. I remember how excited I was when he took me with him for the first time. I was only eight years old and everything was a big adventure. 10 The bus was full of travellers and stopped at every village on the way. It rolled noisily down the mountain roads and turned many

corners above narrow valleys until it got to the plain. That took
four hours.

On the plain I saw wide, flat fields. People were working in them.   15
Some of them waved as we passed, and I waved back. Then at last
we came to the town. It was never a big place, but to me it had more
houses than there were stars in the sky.

Below are some statements relating to the passage. Some are true (T)
in terms of the passage, while others are false (F). Mark them
appropriately, and if a statement is false, say why.

a. ☐ It was a hard journey from the village to the big town.

b. ☐ Nowadays, buses can go right to the village.

c. ☐ The writer's father went to the town to buy things.

d. ☐ The writer was still a child when his father took him to the
town for the first time.

e. ☐ The road out of the hills was straight.

f. ☐ The bus took four hours to get from the village to the town.

g. ☐ The town was in a hilly place.

h. ☐ The writer thought that the town was very big.

2.2 Spelling:
using *y* and *ie*

Look at these four pieces from the passage:

1 In those days, the *journey* ... was not an *easy*   (lines 1–2)
one.

2 Nowadays, the villagers have a much *easier*   (line 5)
life.

3 ... and we *carried* everything ...   (lines 7–8)

4 ... above the narrow *valleys* ...   (line 13)

The *italicized* words in all four pieces follow certain English spelling
rules. These rules concern whether or not a final *y* changes into *ie*.
Below is a list of words. Suffixes (like *-ed*, *-er*, *-est*, *-ly* and *-s*) can be
added to most (but *not* all) of these words. Mark the words which
must change their *y* into *ie*, and add an example of this happening.
Where a word never changes, simply put an 'X'. (The rules for

making these changes are given in the answer section of this unit, in case you need to study them.)

a.	way	e.	day	i.	donkey	m.	lonely
b.	lazy	f.	early	j.	rocky	n.	worry
c.	monkey	g.	friendly	k.	many	o.	necessary
d.	party	h.	every	l.	sky	p.	money

2.3 Grammar and structure: Kinds of sentences

Basically, there are three kinds of sentence in English: simple, compound, and complex.

1 The simple sentence

This type of sentence expresses one idea, or provides one piece of information. It has only one finite verb. Here are four simple sentences taken from the passage:

There *was* no motor road to the village in those days.	(line 4)
That *took* four hours.	(lines 13–14)
On the plain I *saw* wide, flat fields.	(line 15)
People *were working* in them.	(line 15)

2 The compound sentence

This type of sentence consists in effect of two simple sentences *co-ordinated*, that is, joined together by such conjunctions as *and*, *but* and *while*. There are two basic types:

with one subject and two verbs (but usually no comma)	The bus *was* full of travellers and *stopped* at every village on the way. (lines 11–12)
with two subjects, or a repeated subject, and two verbs (usually with a comma)	I *was* only eight years old at the time, and everything *was* a big adventure. (line 10)

3 The complex sentence

This type of sentence consists of two or more parts called *clauses*.
The relationship between clauses is not equal, as with the parts of
compound sentences. The *main* (or *principal*) *clause* is very much like
a simple sentence, while the other clause or clauses are *dependent* (or
subordinate). These dependent clauses are joined to the main clause
by means of connecting words or phrases, such as the conjunctions
although, *because*, *if*, *when*, etc. Each clause has one finite verb, and
dependent clauses like these serve to express things like reasons,
conditions, concessions, times of action, and so on. An example from
the passage is:

> I *remember* how excited I *was* when he *took* me   (lines 8–10)
> with him for the first time.
>
> conjunctions: *how*, *when*

Note Combinations of compound and complex also occur. In the
passage you will find several compound-complex sentences like this:

> It *rolled* noisily down the mountain roads and   (lines 12–14)
> *turned* many corners above the narrow valleys
> until it *got* to the plain.
>
> co-ordinating conjunction: *and*
> subordinating conjunction: *until*

Analysis and synthesis:
First stage

Number the sentences in the passage about a journey, then study
each sentence, noting the finite verbs and conjunctions, and deciding
whether a sentence is simple, compound, complex or compound-
complex.

Analysis and synthesis:
Second stage

In this section you will make your own compound and complex sentences. Study the examples and then work through the material that follows.

Example 1   In those days, there was no motor road.   **but**
              Nowadays, there is.

    ▷   In those days, there was no motor road, but
              nowadays there is.

Example 2   Nowadays, the people have an easier life. The   **because**
              motor road goes all the way to the village.

    ▷   Nowadays, the people have an easier life, because
              the motor road goes all the way to the village.

a.   At that time there was no railway. There is   **but**
      now.

b.   There was a bus three times a week. It was   **and**
      necessary to walk a few kilometres to the bus
      station.

c.   Cats are independent animals. They have their   **and**
      own private lives.

d.   Cats are not completely domestic. They still   **because**
      like to hunt and wander about.

e.   There was a train every day. It was necessary   **but**
      for us to walk a few miles to the station. We   **because**
      lived out of town.

f.   I was very young at the time. I got very   **and**
      excited. He asked me to go with him.   **when**

g.   People usually refer to cats as female. This is   **that**
      an interesting fact.
      (*Begin*: It is an interesting fact . . .)

h.   Some people spoke to us. We were walking   **as**
      past the shops. They wanted to sell us things.   **because**

i.   It is true. Buses go regularly to all the villages. **that**
      They bring people to work in the city.   **and**

j.   Women are called 'cats'. They say unkind   **if**
      things about other women. Men are not called   **but**
      'cats'. They say unkind things about other   **if**
      men.

k.   My father went to town. He sold things. He often needed money to buy new tools and materials.

when
because

l.   My father lived in a village. He did not like big towns. He often had to go to the nearest city. He could sell his goods there.

although
and
where

Analysis and synthesis:
Third stage

The table which follows contains the elements of a passage on a journey, similar to the one at the beginning of this unit. Combine the material on the left with the material on the right, by means of the conjunctions in the middle, laying out your work carefully.

First statements	Conjunctions	Second statements
In those days, it was necessary to travel on foot or on horseback.	because	There were no trains, buses or cars in that part of the country.
I remember.	when and	I was about nine years old. My father took me with him down the mountain to the big town on the plain.
We travelled all day.	until where	We came to a small inn on the edge of the town. My father usually stayed (there).
We had a good meal.	and or because	(We) slept soundly that night. At least, I did. I was so tired.
In the morning, early, my father took me with him to the market.	where and	He did all his business. I learned a lot by watching him bargaining.

2.4 Punctuation:
Using commas

The table below shows some ways in which commas are used in the passage:

Examples	Uses
1 There was a bus twice a week, and it was necessary to walk three kilometres to where the bus waited. (lines 2–4) It was never a big place, but to me it had more houses than there were stars in the sky. (lines 16–17)	The comma separates parts of compound sentences.
2 ... down the steep, rocky path ... (line 8) ... I saw wide, flat fields. (line 15)	The comma separates items in a list.
3 In those days, the journey ... (line 1) Nowadays, the villagers ... (line 5)	The comma separates a special word or phrase from the rest of a sentence.

These are three typical uses of commas. The comma is not always easy to use in English. Absolute recommendations are not possible, but the following points are important:

1   Periods (or full-stops) are essential, but commas are often optional.

2   Basically, commas are used to separate pieces of information inside a sentence. If, however, one piece of information is intended to flow smoothly into another, then it may not be a good idea to put a comma between them.

3   The separation of one piece of information inside a sentence from another is often (in English at least) a matter of personal choice. The separation may depend on what a writer wants to emphasize.

4   When shorter sentences are combined into longer ones (usually, simple into compound and complex), periods tend to be replaced by commas.

5   Too many commas on a page are probably worse than too few. In the final version of a piece of writing there may well be fewer commas than when the writer started.

Punctuation work:
First stage

The passage below has periods and capital letters, but no commas. Read it, considering where you would like to put commas, and why. After the passage you will see six phrases taken from it, each followed by a comma. These show where I would put the commas. Compare your own approaches with mine.

> Elephants are very large animals. They are wild animals like lions but in parts of Asia people use them to pull heavy loads. They like to move about in herds. The elephant eats plants unlike the lion which eats meat. Ancient peoples in Asia and Africa used elephants in their wars but the elephants often got excited and attacked both their friends and their enemies. In battle the elephant was therefore not a very safe weapon.

/wild animals,/   /like lions,/   /eats plants,/
/unlike the lion,/   /in their wars,/   /In battle,/

This is the minimum number of commas needed. A good case can also be made, however, for the following:

/got excited,/   /, therefore,/

Punctuation work:
Second stage

The passage below has no periods, capital letters or commas. Instead, slashes (/) are used to show that a period or a comma is needed. Punctuate the passage.

> cats are independent animals/ dogs/ however/ are not/ dogs generally like to be part of the family/ while cats like to keep some secrets of their own/ domestic cats still have a lot in common with their bigger sisters/ the lion and the tiger/ but most domestic dogs do not have much in common with their wild relative/ the wolf/ in ancient times/ the cat was a goddess/ but the dog was a worker/ protecting sheep and the home/

Punctuation work:
Third stage

Here is a passage without any marks or aids of any kind. Study it, then punctuate it fully.

at that time people were travelling every day from our village to the big city they did this because there was no work for them in the village but most people could find some kind of work in the city I remember very clearly the day when I first went to the city to look for a job I tried to look brave but inside me I was feeling pretty nervous I walked through the city all day going to many places I tried shops hotels factories a government office the bus station and the railway station but there were no jobs I was unlucky that day

2.5 Grammar: Definite and indefinite articles

The following points about articles are important in the writing of English:

1   The definite article is used to show that someone or something is known or has already been mentioned:

   ... *the* journey from our village in *the* hills to *the* nearest big town ...   (lines 1–2)

   There was a bus twice a week, and it was necessary to walk about three kilometres to where *the* bus waited.   (lines 2–4)

2   The indefinite article means the same as the number *one* but belongs to a different system:

a/an	one
some	two
many	three
more	four
most *etc*	five *etc*

   Compare:
   He bought *a* book.   (a simple statement of fact)
   He bought *one* book.   (not two books, or three ...)

3   Countable nouns (that is, nouns that take numbers: *one man, two men, three men*, etc) need the indefinite article, but uncountable nouns do not: *Do you like wine? Have some wine.* **Note**, however, that sometimes uncountable nouns can be used countably: *This is a nice Spanish wine.*

4   Abstract nouns like *beauty* or *love* do not need a definite article unless the noun is made specific: '*the* beauty that one sees in a sunset; *the* love of a good woman'.

5   In the passage about a journey *the* occurs sixteen times. Only one occurrence relates to something being mentioned before (lines 2–3: *a* bus . . . *the* bus). On all the other occasions, *the* relates to known or specific matters (*the* journey; *the* hills; *the* nearest big town; *the* village; *the* villagers; *the* town (twice); *the* steep, rocky path; in *the* morning; for *the* first time; *the* bus; on *the* way; *the* mountain roads; *the* plain (twice).

The best way to master the use of the articles is simply practice. Below are two passages which should now be quite familiar (more or less). Decide whether a definite or an indefinite article is needed in the each blank space, or whether you should put an 'X' to show that no article is needed.

Passage 1

In those days, (1)_____ journey from our village in (2)_____ hills to (3)_____ nearest big town was not (4)_____ easy one. There was (5)_____ bus twice (6)_____ week, and it was necessary to walk (7)_____ kilometre or more to where (8)_____ bus waited. At that time there was only (9)_____ dirt track to (10)_____ village, but now there is (11)_____ proper motor road. Nowadays, (12)_____ villagers have (13)_____ much easier life.

Passage 2

(14)_____ friend of mine has (15)_____ cat called (16)_____ Cleopatra. This cat sometimes goes away for (17)_____ weeks, and no one sees her or knows where she is. Occasionally, however, my friend finds her sitting on (18)_____ wall in (19)_____ moonlight, (20)_____ miles from (21)_____ home. She comes down from (22)_____ wall, rubs herself against my friend to say (23)_____ 'hullo', then walks away again. She comes back about (24)_____ week later, quite happy, in her own good time. Cleopatra is (25)_____ independent animal. She is (26)_____ cat who knows her own mind, not (27)_____ kind of (28)_____ animal who really belongs to anybody.

2.6 Vocabulary: Forming words

Adjectives can be formed from nouns in English in many ways. Two common ways are to use the suffixes *-y* and *-ly* with a range of everyday words. The rules are:

1   *-y* is added to the names of common substances, objects and things that are experienced:

rock : rocky   (= full of rocks; like rocks or rock)
noise : noisy   (= having or producing a lot of noise)
hill : hilly   (= full of hills)
rain : rainy   (= having a lot of rain)

2   *-ly* is added to time words and to certain family and personal words:

week : weekly   (= happening once a week/ every week)
day : daily   (= happening every day)
father : fatherly   (= like a father in some way, usually good)
man : manly   (= like a man; having the proper qualities of a man)

Now study the example below and complete the exercise.

Example   The land near the village is very _____.   **hill**
   ▷   The land near the village is very hilly.

a.   He makes _____ visits to the town on business.   **month**

b.   The beach was _____ in some places, rocky in others.   **sand**

c.   There was a _____ white material on the table.   **powder**

d.   He gets annual or _____ payments.   **year**

e.   He spoke to her in a _____ way, trying to help.   **brother**

f.   The land is rather _____ between here and the river.   **stone**

g.   He is a good man, with a very _____ manner.   **saint**

h.   The food was far too _____ for my taste.   **salt**

i.   It was a _____ day and we could not see much.   **fog**

j.   They have meetings every three months, and these _____ meetings are important.   **quarter**

2.7 Controlled composition: 'Journeys'

Below are two sets of words which can be turned into descriptions of journeys, one in Scotland and the other in France. Create the passages, each in one well-organized paragraph, taking care with punctuation, layout, spelling and grammar.

Scotland

1 I/remember/how/pleased/I/be/when/my/father/take/me/Fort William/first/time

2 I/be/about/twelve/year/old/time/and/have/never/be/in/Scottish Highlands/before

3 we/travel/bus/Glasgow

4 journey/begin/nine/o'clock/morning/and/take/several/hour

5 it/be/very/interesting/because/bus/pass/through/such/beautiful/country

6 on/way/I/see/mountain/forest/river/and/'lochs'/which/be/Scottish/name/lake

7 when/at/last/we/reach/Fort William/I/be/ready/for/good/lunch/and/then/afternoon/explore/town

France

1 I/remember/how/excited/I/be/when/my/mother/take/me/Paris/first/visit

2 I/be/not/more/than/eleven/then

3 we/go/there/express/train/Bordeaux

4 train/leave/eight/morning/and/journey/last/several/hour

5 it/be/interesting/because/I/be/able/see/many/place/that/I/never/see/before

6 we/have/meal/train/and/we/talk/several/people/who/live/work/Paris

7 when/at/length/we/get/there/I/feel/rather/small/such/big/city/and/be/little/worried/by/all/traffic

8 it/be/however/memorable/trip

2.8   Editing a text: 'Journey down the Zaire'

The following passage is a brief report on real-life journeys made by boat down the river Zaire in Africa. It is not, however, quite ready for publication. Edit the text, looking for the following errors:

1 missing article
1 article too many
2 tense mistakes
2 singular/plural mistakes
2 mistakes omitting commas
1 apostrophe mistake
1 quotation mistake

> In late 19th century, an American journalist called Henry Stanley travelled widely in the Central Africa. Wherever he went he took with him a small wooden boat that could be taken to pieces, and on this boat he journey down the great river that was then called the Congo but is now call the Zaire.
>
> A hundred year later in early 1975, a group of British soldiers and scientist repeated Stanley's historic journey, using modern equipment and inflatable boats with engines. This bold expedition collected enough interesting material to keep scientists busy for at least five years.
>
> About Stanley the leader of the expedition, Colonel John Snell said: 'I admire that man very much. I dont know how he managed to get through.

UNIT 3

3.1 Comprehension and composition model: 'The Warship'

Original painting of *HMS Ulysses* in the North Atlantic, by Paul Wright.

Here is a short passage about a book by the novelist Alistair Maclean. Note how it is laid out on the page, and then read it twice.

> The original Ulysses was an ancient Greek hero, but Maclean's Ulysses is a ship.
>
> The novel entitled *HMS Ulysses* is about men, ships and war in the awful conditions of the North Atlantic and Arctic, and does not have a happy ending. If you like happy endings, this is just not the book for you. The action takes place during the Second World War and centres on the *Ulysses*, just one ship among the many ships that guarded the Allied supply lines in the North Atlantic. Its story suggests that war is pointless and wasteful, destroying good men and good ships to no purpose.
>
> Maclean describes how the *Ulysses* and her sailors die in the ice, fire and water at the top of the world, attacked by both human and natural enemies during a terrible northern winter. At the end of the book, he describes how the warship went on through terrific seas, covered with ice and badly damaged, but still moving at great speed. Then her magazine blew up, blowing a great hole in her bows, so that the sea rushed in. She drove herself onward and downward into the rolling waters, 'to the black floor of the Arctic', her great engines still turning – and took every man with her.

5

10

15

Below are some statements relating to the passage. Some are true (T) in terms of the passage, while others are false (F). Mark them appropriately, and if a statement is false, say why.

a. ☐ The ancient Ulysses was a ship.

b. ☐ Many ships guarded the Allied supply lines.

c. ☐ Maclean suggests that war is a waste of people and resources.

d. ☐ *HMS Ulysses* carried supplies.

e. ☐ The ship was covered in ice when it blew up.

f. ☐ The ship sank because the ice made a great hole in its bows.

g. ☐ The engines of the *Ulysses* pushed it under the water.

h. ☐ No one was saved.

3.2 Spelling: Changing words

Each of the sentences below has a blank space in it. Beside each sentence you will find a word which can be used to complete the blank, but the word must be changed slightly in order to do so. Study the example, then complete the sentences.

Example	The original Ulysses was a man, but Maclean's Ulysses _____ a ship.	**be**
▷	The original Ulysses was a man, but Maclean's Ulysses is a ship.	

a.	The story _____ not have a happy ending.	**do**
b.	The man was _____ of thirst in the desert.	**die**
c.	Alistair Maclean has _____ many novels.	**write**
d.	It must have _____ a lot of courage to be a sailor in the Second World War.	**take**
e.	The story is about the _____ of a ship.	**destroy**
f.	The ship went on through _____ seas.	**terror**
g.	Is there a lot of _____ in the novel?	**describe**
h.	The captain told his men to stop _____.	**fire**
i.	In winter the roads are often very _____.	**ice**
j.	It was summer, but the weather was quite _____.	**winter**
k.	He has _____ a car for many years.	**drive**
l.	The ship was _____ to pieces.	**blow**

3.3 Grammar and structure: The relative pronouns *that, which* and *who(m)*

Study the example below, then change the sentences in the same way.

Example 1	There were many warships. These warships guarded the Allied supply lines.	
▷	There were many warships that guarded the Allied supply lines.	

a. There were many dogs. These dogs guarded the camp.

b. I saw several houses. The houses were for sale.

c. He wrote a book. The book describes war in the Atlantic.

d. In those days, there were a lot of ships. The ships sailed back and forth between the islands.

e. He made many journeys. These journeys took him to the farthest corners of the earth.

In this exercise you have used the word *that* as a relative pronoun, a means of combining two simple sentences into one complex sentence. You can, however make the same combinations with *which*, and the result will be more formal:

Example 2 There were many warships which guarded the Allied supply lines.

Re-express the sentences a–e using *which*, then study the next example.

Example 3 The ships were in great danger. These ships guarded the Allied supply lines.

▷ The ships $\begin{matrix} that \\ which \end{matrix}$ guarded the Allied supply lines were in great danger.

Now change the following sentences in the same way, first using the less formal *that*, then the more formal *which*.

f. The dogs were dangerous. These dogs guarded the camp.

g. The book is in the library. It describes the war.

h. The letters are on the table. They must be posted today.

i. The houses are in the village. These houses must be sold soon.

j. The story describes a ship called the *Ulysses*. It was written by Alistair Maclean.

You may have noticed that no commas have been used so far in the examples. You therefore should not have used commas in the exercise sentences. The use of commas in such sentences generally changes the meaning completely. Below you will find a table which shows Example 3 again, first without commas and then with commas. An explanation of the different meanings is added on the right-hand side:

Punctuation	*Which* sentences	Meanings
without commas	The ships which guarded the Allied supply lines were in great danger.	These ships and only these ships were in great danger. Other ships in other places were not.
with commas	The ships, which guarded the Allied supply lines, were in great danger.	There were some ships, these ships guarded the Allied supply lines, and they were *all* in great danger.

Using the table to help you, look again at the sentences listed f to j. Consider them without and then with commas, and think about the ways in which the meanings change. (Further reference is made to this point in Section 3.5, Note, and in Section 3.6, Point 3.)

In the above exercises, the relative pronouns *that* and *which* relate to the subjects of sentences or clauses. In the following examples, however, the pronouns relate to objects:

Example 4   I saw the boat. They had built it themselves.

     ▷   I saw the boat which they had built themselves.   **formal**

               that they had built themselves.   **informal**

               they had built themselves.   **very informal (no pronoun)**

Now, for each of the following pairs of sentences, provide three complex sentences as in the example.

k.   This is the work. He used to do it.

l.   She works in the library. I showed you it yesterday.

m.   That is the ship. He mentioned it last night.

n.   This is the cat. My friend calls it/her Cleopatra.

o.   They showed us the map. He used that map when he travelled down the Zaire river.

For persons, of course, the relative pronoun is *who(m)*. This pronoun also works in the same way:

Example 5   This is the man. He came yesterday.

     ▷   This is the man who came yesterday.

Example 6   This is the man. You mentioned him yesterday.

     ▷   This is the man whom you mentioned yesterday.

               that you mentioned yesterday.

               you mentioned yesterday.

Sometimes, the relative pronoun relates to a special prepositional phrase. This can result in four possibilities when simple sentences are combined:

Example 7   That is the ship. He was writing about it.

      ▷   That is the ship about which he was writing.   **very formal**

                         which he was writing about.   **quite formal**

                         that he was writing about.   **informal**

                         he was writing about.   **very informal (no pronoun)**

Re-express these sentences in the same way:

p.   This is the book. I was telling you about it.

q.   That is the village. He goes back to that village every year.

r.   The *Ulysses* was a warship. Many terrible things happened to it.

s.   The animals were very interesting. He referred to them in his book.

t.   The journey was long and difficult. He has just returned from that journey.

3.4 Grammar and structure: Analysis of sentences

Number the sentences in the passage about the *Ulysses*, then study each sentence, noting the finite verbs and conjunctions, and deciding whether a sentence is simple, compound, complex or compound-complex. (If you wish, you can try to lay the whole passage out like the material in Section 2.3, Third Stage. The material will be found, laid out in this way, in the answer section.)

3.5 Grammar and style: Using participles

It is possible to make your style more interesting by using participial expressions instead of clauses beginning with relative pronouns. Study the examples and change the sentences accordingly.

Example 1   There were many ships that guarded the supply lines.

▷   There were many ships guarding the supply lines.

   a.   There were many soldiers who guarded the camp.
   b.   He read the book that described war in the North Atlantic.
   c.   She read an account that showed how the ship sank.
   d.   There are not very many places that provide this kind of information.
   e.   There were a lot of ships that needed urgent help.

Example 2   The ships which guarded the supply lines were in great danger.

▷   The ships guarding the supply lines were in great danger.

   f.   The dogs that guarded the camp were dangerous.
   g.   The book which describes the war fully is in the library.
   h.   Offices that provide this kind of help are not common.
   i.   Aircraft that fly across the Atlantic need plenty of fuel.
   j.   Work which provides good pay and conditions is not always easy to find.

Example 3   The ships which were guarded by the warships sailed on to safety.

▷   The ships guarded by the warships sailed on to safety.

   k.   The camp which was guarded by the dogs was never attacked.
   l.   Aircraft which are provided with plenty of fuel fly across the Atlantic every day.
   m.   Books which have been written by people like Alistair Maclean are usually exciting to read.
   n.   It is not pleasant to read about ships or cities that have been destroyed as a result of war.
   o.   Maclean's book, which is described as one of the most exciting sea stories ever written, is in our local library.

Note   You may have noticed once again that no commas were used in the examples above, and were not needed in any exercise sentence until the last. As with the material in Section 3.3, the addition of commas generally changes the meaning of a sentence completely. Below you will find a table which shows Example 3 again, first without and then with commas. An explanation of the different meanings is added on the right-hand side:

Punctuation	Use of participles	Meanings
without commas	The ships guarded by the warships sailed on to safety.	These ships and only these ships sailed on to safety. Other ships were not guarded and were not so lucky.
with commas	The ships, guarded by the warships, sailed on to safety.	There were some ships, these ships were guarded by the warships, and all of them sailed on to safety. We are not concerned with any other ships.

If you wish, you can use commas in the sentences k−o, and think about the ways in which the meanings change. No comments are offered in the answer section. (Further reference is made to this point in Section 3.6, Point 3.)

3.6 Punctuation:
Further uses of the comma

Essentially, commas in English express some kind of separation and interruption. If the writer feels a real need for a brief interruption, he or she will use a comma. If a sense of continuous flow is more useful, then no comma is inserted. In this connection, these six points should be helpful:

1   Co-ordinating conjunctions bring simple sentences together as compound sentences. In such combinations, a comma is useful to show that the sentence contains a 'change of direction':

The original Ulysses was an ancient Greek hero, but Maclean's Ulysses is a ship.

It is common, however, to leave the comma out if the two parts (or clauses) have the same subject or are very short:

I slept well last night but still feel tired this morning.

They missed the train but there was a bus going the same way.

Again, it is usually necessary to exercise judgement in sentences containing options (that is, several possibilities). The examples below show how a writer can emphasize different things simply by organizing the commas differently:

> They missed the train, but there was a bus going the same way, so they took that.

> They missed the train, but there was a bus going the same way so they took that.

> They missed the train but there was a bus going the same way, so they took that.

The writer might avoid commas completely, in order to suggest speed and continuity:

> They missed the train but there was a bus going the same way so they took that.

Or, quite possibly, in informal writing, there could be periods instead of commas, producing a short, sharp effect:

> They missed the train. But there was a bus going the same way. So they took that.

This last arrangement does not exhaust the possibilities.

2 Subordinating conjunctions bring simple sentences together as complex sentences. The same principles apply as for co-ordinating conjunctions, but there has been a traditional preference for commas in front of such conjunctions or after dependent (subordinate) clauses:

> I will go, if you will tell me where to go.

> If you will tell me where to go, I will go.

> The bus was not ready to leave, although the timetable said that it would leave at two o'clock.

(**Note** that no comma is placed in front of *where* or *that*, because it would destroy the necessary continuity.)

> Although the timetable said that the bus would leave at two o'clock, it was not ready to leave.

3 An interesting distinction is made between two special kinds of relative clause (that is, clauses introduced by relative pronouns). Compare the following:

> My uncle who lives in Brazil is coming to see us.

> My uncle, who lives in Brazil, is coming to see us.

In the first example, the writer suggests continuity and that there are several uncles, only one of whom lives in Brazil. In the second example, however, the writer interrupts the flow, making it clear that there is only one uncle, and he lives in Brazil. (In technical terms, the first of these examples is called a restrictive or defining relative clause, while the second is called a non-restrictive or non-defining relative clause.)

4 Certain phrases, especially those containing participles, are followed by a comma:

Sailing north, they at length reached ice.

Having sailed for days, they were glad to see land again.

He sailed immediately, hoping to avoid the storm.

Worried, he looked at the stormy clouds ahead.

5 Similarly, certain special words are set off by means of a comma:

John, come here!

Can I help you, sir?

Oh, what a funny idea!

Basically, there is no difference.

Nevertheless, it is time to finish the work.

6 Commas are used to mark off special dates, addresses, titles, etc:

He was born on April 14th, 1960.

She spoke to Alistair Maclean, the novelist.

He lives at 440 Northview, Sutton, Essex.

Below are two passages for punctuation:

Passage 1

people love stories children like listening to stories at bedtime and adults like reading them or watching them on television there is a large market in storybooks almost everywhere in the world thousands of stories for all tastes but ultimately only a few basic plots new books and films tell the worlds old stories in endless new ways hms ulysses for example is the old theme of men fighting both natural and human enemies even when such men are defeated they have in a sense still won their battles because we do not forget them writers like alistair maclean also take old names like ulysses names which have their own special power and use them in new ways giving them fresh significance

Passage 2

in the late 19th century an american journalist called henry stanley travelled widely in central africa wherever he went he took with him a small wooden boat that could be taken to pieces and on this boat he journeyed down the great river then called the congo but

51

nowadays known as the zaire a hundred years later in early 1975 a group of british soldiers and scientists repeated stanleys historic journey using modern equipment and inflatable boats with engines this expedition was led by colonel john snell a great admirer of stanley the group did not find the trip easy and snell wondered how on earth stanley had managed it at all they were chased by animals fell sick with fever and found the river currents dangerous snell commented afterwards that sometimes the river seemed alive its great whirlpools often threatening to swallow them up

3.7 Vocabulary: Forming words

Adjectives can be formed from nouns in English in many ways. Two common ways are to use the suffixes *-ful* and *-less*. The rules are:

1   when *-ful* is added it indicates in a positive way the presence of a quality, ability, etc, while the addition of *-less* negatively suggests the absence of that quality, ability, etc:

use: useful (= having a use)
    useless (= having no use)

2   Some nouns take both suffixes, while others, for obvious reasons, need only the one or the other:

skill: skilful (*British*), skillful (*American*)
    (= having skill)
head: headless (= having no head)

Now study the example below and complete the sentences, either with an adjective, as above, or with an adverb formed from an adjective by adding *-ly*.

Example   Most of the machines are old, but they are still very _____.   **use**

▷   Most of the machines are old, but they are still very useful.

a.   The doctor said sadly that the patient's condition was _____.   **hope**

b.   They used their money so _____ that now they do not have much left.   **waste**

c.   The journey was long, and seemed _____.   **end**

d.   In summer he prefers _____ shirts.   **sleeve**

e.   She works hard and very _____ .   **purpose**

f.   When they lost their jobs, life became quite   **meaning**
     _____ .

g.   Poisonous insects are _____ creatures.   **harm**

h.   These books are valuable to me, but are quite   **value**
     _____ to most other people.

i.   Some nations are more _____ than others,   **power**
     because of their armies and warships. Weaker
     nations may well feel quite _____ against
     them.

3.8 Vocabulary:
The right word in the right place

In the passage below there are ten blank spaces, numbered
appropriately. Following the passage are ten sets of three words each,
also numbered. Choose the word from each set that best fits the
passage. The first most suitable word is underlined for you, as an aid.

HMS Ulysses is the (1)_____ of a ship in time of war, a ship in
her finest (2)_____ . She was destroyed while (3)_____ the
work for which she had been built. The men on board faced
(4)_____ human and natural (5)_____ , and it is difficult to
decide which were (6)_____ . The reader finds it hard to
(7)_____ the characters in the story, from the most important
officer down to the (8)_____ significant young sailor. The tale is
told in a (9)_____ that gives the reader no (10)_____ at all
when the time comes to close the book.

  (1)   description, story, history
  (2)   hour, day, time
  (3)   carrying, making, doing
  (4)   also, both, either
  (5)   fights, disasters, enemies
  (6)   bad, worse, worst
  (7)   remember, forget, ignore
  (8)   little, less, least
  (9)   way, fashion, means
 (10)   pleasure, comfort, warning

3.9 Controlled composition: 'The Narrow Escape'

Create a passage of one or more paragraphs from the material printed below. Keep the story in the past tenses and take due care with the spelling, punctuation, layout and grammar.

1 Northern Queen/sail/in/Arctic Ocean/as/part/scientific/survey
2 she/work/far/north/than/other/two/ship/in/group
3 it/be/now/late/in/year/and/there/be/still/great/deal/work/be/do
4 captain/therefore/take/risk
5 he/delay/as/long/possible/area/although/winter/ice/begin/form
6 he/delay/too/long/however/as/ice/begin/surround/ship
7 soon/there/be/no/way/out/any/direction
8 after/several/more/day/Northern Queen/be/complete/trap
9 captain/send/urgent/radio/message/help/because/there/be/now/real/danger/weight/ice/would/crush/ship
10 rescue/reach/they/air/just/time/however/save/crew/although/unfortunate/vessel/could/not/be/save

3.10 Editing a text: 'Animals'

There are a variety of faults in the following passage. Edit them.

Every species of animal has its own character. Cats for example, are more independant than dogs and has their own private lives, while dogs are, on the whole, more domestic and usefull than cats. Horses, in the past have been even more useful to the human race than dogs, but it probably true to say that, of all animal, cow is the most valuable. Cow provides a whole range of foodstuffs: milk, butter, cheese, yohgurt and cream, and many people also eat its meat. In India, however most people do no eat beef and will do anything to avoid killing cow.

It is difficult to imagine the wild ancestors of many of our domestic animals. We can, however, look at tiger to see what a large wild cat is like and at the wolf to see what the original ancestral form of a spaniel or poodle really was. The human race today no longer live closely associated with animal life, and many of us come close to real wild creature only when we go to zoo. Unless of course we consider some human beings are wild rather than domestic. If that is true, then we often meet wild creature driving cars dangerously or causing other kind of trouble.

UNIT 4

4.1 Comprehension and composition model: 'The Clever Queen'

Engraving taken from *The Arabian Nights*. It shows Shahrezad and the King.

Here is a short passage about a king and a queen, adapted from the collection of stories called *The Thousand and One Nights*. Note how it is laid out on the page, and read it twice.

Shahriyar, the King of Persia, did not like women.

His first queen had deceived him badly, and he was consequently determined that no woman would ever deceive him again. To make sure of this, he took a new queen every evening – and had her executed in the morning. 5

The turn came of the beautiful Shahrezad, who did not however intend to die so easily. She was also determined to put an end to the king's savage practices. Consequently, she arranged for her younger sister to come to the palace early, to ask a favour from Shahriyar. The favour was simple enough: 10 Shahrezad was a skilled teller of tales, and her sister would ask to hear one more story before the executioner did his work.

The king listened with amusement to Shahrezad's sister's request and then to the tale itself, which slowly, however, began to gain his attention. It was still unfinished when the time of 15 execution arrived, and this made the king angry, because he wanted both to hear the end of this intriguing tale and to watch the execution. He could not, however, have both.

Shahriyar chose to hear the end of the story, but the matter was not quite as simple as he expected. As soon as she finished 20 her first story, Queen Shahrezad began a second tale that grew quite naturally out of the first. The king found this continuation just as interesting as the earlier story had been, and listened on – and on. One story became another, one day became another, and the executioner remained without any work to do. 25

The king spared his queen's life, as he waited for the end that never seemed to come. For a thousand and one nights, so we are told, the clever queen spun her web of tales, and in the time that it took to tell them King Shahriyar grew to love her and, when at last the stories ended, he had no wish to send for the executioner 30 ever again.

Below are some statements relating to the passage. Some are true (T) in terms of the passage, while others are false (F). Mark them appropriately, and if a statement is false, say why.

a. ☐ The King of Persia's name was Shahrezad.

b. ☐ The king liked to deceive women.

c. ☐ Shahrezad knew that she would die if she became queen.

d. ☐ The king was angry because he was not able to execute Shahrezad at the right time.

e. ☐ The king intended to execute his queen as soon as the story ended.

f. ☐ We know that the stories continued for exactly a thousand and one nights.

g. ☐ The queen lived on because she had an endless supply of stories to tell the king.

h. ☐ Whenever she finished a story, the queen had already started the next.

4.2 Spelling:
Commonly misspelt words

Below are two lists of words that are often misspelled. The first list consists of words containing 'ie', while the second consists of words containing 'ei'. Memorize how they look, getting a friend to test you.

ie words	ei words
achieve	conceit
ancient	conceive
anxiety	deceit
belief	deceive
believe	foreign
chief	leisure
conscience	receipt
relief	receive
relieve	seize
siege	seizure
society	

4.3 Grammar:
Contrasts

In the table below you will find information about some important ways of expressing contrasts in English:

Contrast words	Examples	Usage
but	The king was angry, but he did not kill the queen.	general and informal
however	The king was angry. He did not, however, kill the queen.	more formal and emphatic
	The king was angry. However, he did not kill the queen.	more emphatic still
still	The king was angry. Still, he did not kill the queen.	informal concession
even so	The king was angry. Even so, he did not kill the queen.	emphatic concession
	The king was angry, but even so he did not kill the queen.	
nevertheless	The king was angry. He nevertheless did not kill the queen.	formal and emphatic concession
	The king was angry. Nevertheless, he did not kill the queen.	more emphatic still
although, though	(Al)Though the King was angry, he did not kill the queen.	alternative form for concession
even though	Even though the king was angry, he did not kill the queen.	more emphatic

Practise these variations by transforming the following sentences:

a.   Cats are domestic animals, but they are not so completely domestic as dogs.

b.   The ancient Egyptians were the first people to keep cats, but they did not keep them as pets.

c.   Horses are useful animals, but they are not more useful than cows.

d.   It was not a big town, but to the child it seemed to have more houses than there were stars in the sky.

e.   The original Ulysses was an ancient Greek hero, but Maclean's Ulysses is a ship.

4.4 Grammar:
Reasons, results and consequences

In the table below you will find information about various ways of expressing reasons and their results or consequences:

Words expressing result/consequence	Examples	Usage
so	The king did not want to be deceived again, so he executed one queen after another.	general and informal
therefore	The king did not want to be deceived again. He therefore executed one queen after another.	more formal
	The king did not want to be deceived again. Therefore he executed one queen after another.	more emphatic
consequently	The king did not want to be deceived again. He consequently executed one queen after another.	more formal still
	The king did not want to be deceived again. Consequently, he executed one queen after another.	more emphatic still

Practise these variations by transforming these sentences:

a. The queen wanted to live, so she told endless stories.

b. She expected to meet him in town at 12 o'clock, so she left home at 11.30.

c. He did not want to be sent away, so he tried even harder to please them.

d. The sailors did not want to be trapped by the ice, so they sent urgent radio messages for help.

e. The travellers decided that it would be easier to reach their destination by river than by road, so they began looking for someone with a suitable boat.

The same relationship between clauses in a sentence can be expressed as a reason and its consequence. Study the example below, then re-express sentences a–e in the same way, labelling your new sentences f, g, h, i and j.

Example The king did not want to be deceived again, so he executed one queen after another.

▷ Because the king did not want to be deceived again, he executed one queen after another.

The king executed one queen after another because he did not want to be deceived again.

The writer may, however, wish to emphasize a desired result rather than a reason. To do this, he or she could choose from among the following:

Words for desired results	Examples	Usage
so that	The king executed one queen after another, so that he would not be deceived again. /So that he would not be deceived again, the king executed one queen after another.	general
to make sure (that)	The king executed one queen after another to make sure that he was not **or** would not be deceived again./ To make sure that . . . one queen after another.	less formal, but also emphatic
in order that	The king executed one queen after another in order that he would not be deceived again./ In order that he . . . one queen after another.	more formal

Practise these variations by transforming the following sentences:

k. The queen told endless stories. She did not want to be executed.

l. He took a taxi. He wanted to get to the station on time.

m. She worked very hard. She did not want to lose her job.

n. They did the work at night as well as during the day. They wanted to finish it quickly.

o. The sailors sent urgent radio messages for help. They did not want to be trapped by the ice.

Note that it is also possible to use *in order to* together with *make* or *be sure* and also with an infinitive construction:

Examples The king executed one queen after another in order to make sure that he was not deceived again.

The king executed one queen after another in order to be sure that he was not deceived again.

The king executed one queen after another in order not to be deceived again.

4.5 Punctuation:
Parenthesis

Parenthesis, in English, is the insertion of extra material into a sentence in a way which interrupts the flow of that sentence. There are two main reasons for doing this:

1 Distinguishing words and phrases which serve to relate sentences to each other, as in:

> He could not, however, have both.   (line 18)

It is not always necessary, however, to do this. There are examples in the passage (lines 3, 7) where, in order not to spoil the flow of the story, this is *not* done. This kind of parenthesis can occur at the beginning of a sentence too:

> Consequently, she arranged for her   (lines 8–9)
> younger sister to come to the palace early.

2 Adding extra information in the form of what is often called 'an aside'. Asides are usually interesting and are often useful, but they could easily be omitted from a sentence, especially from the grammatical point of view:

> Shahriyar, the King of Persia, did not like women. (line 1)

> For a thousand and one nights, so we are told,   (lines 27–28)
> the clever queen spun her web of tales.

The commonest punctuation marks for parenthesis in English are commas, but brackets and dashes are also frequently used. Consider these variations:

> Shahriyar (the King of Persia) did not like women.

> Shahriyar – the King of Persia – did not like women.

Brackets and dashes are much more powerful devices than commas, and should be used with care. Brackets are common in technical and academic English, while dashes are common in dramatic fiction, journalism, etc:

Brackets

> Maclean's novels (published by Collins) are famous throughout the world.

> Mr Bennet (to the chairman): May I speak now?

> The information (See Table 4) was collected throughout 1979 and 1980.

Dashes

> She watched the train come in – Oh, how happy she was! – and began to run along the platform.

> The car he drove – a shiny new 1984 model – was his most expensive possession.

> One king of Persia – the cruel Shahriyar – treated his wives in a very savage way.

Note   that the single dash can often be used for dramatic effect towards the end of a sentence:

> She drove herself onward and downward into the rolling waters, her great engines still turning – and took every man with her.

Now re-write the following material properly punctuated, each section including a suitable form of parenthesis:

a.   cats are domestic animals like dogs but they are not so completely domestic as dogs

b.   the cat was a god in ancient egypt or more correctly a goddess

c.   cleopatra my friends cat occasionally goes away for weeks and no one knows where she is sometimes however my friend finds her sitting on a wall in the moonlight miles from home

d.   if a woman behaves badly especially towards other women she is called a cat

e.   we had a good meal and slept soundly that night or at least I did because I was so tired

f.   when at length we got there I felt rather small in such a big city as paris and was a little worried by all the traffic it was however a memorable trip

g.   writers like alistair maclean take old names like ulysses names which have their own special power and use them in new ways

h.   a hundred years later in early 1975 a group of british soldiers and scientists repeated stanleys journey down the zaire one of africas greatest rivers travelling in inflatable boats with engines

i.   every species of animal has its own character cats for example are more independent than dogs and have their own private lives while dogs are on the whole more domestic and useful than cats horses in the past have been even more useful to the human race than dogs but it is probably true to say that of all animals the cow has been and still is the most valuable

j.   long ago according to the thousand and one nights there lived in the land of china a tailor called mustafa he was very poor and had few possessions but he did have a son called aladdin mustafa wanted aladdin to learn how to make clothes so that he could be useful in the tailors shop but aladdin did not want to all he wanted to do was to play games in the street with other boys then his father fell ill and died leaving his poor widow to look after everything sometimes she asked her useless son to help her but he never did it is interesting that fate should have given to that most unhelpful child a wonderful lamp that granted him everything he could wish for life is hardly fair

4.6 Vocabulary: The right word in the right place

In the passage below there are ten blank spaces, numbered appropriately. Following the passage are ten sets of three words each, also numbered. Choose the word from each set that best fits the passage.

The stories called *The Thousand and One Nights* are also (1)_____ as *The Arabian Nights*, although many come from Iran and India. The Arab world (2)_____, however, made them famous, and some of the heroes, (3)_____ as Ali Baba and the Sultan Haroun Al-Rashid, are (4)_____ Arab figures. In the story of Ali Baba, forty thieves (5)_____ a surprise attack on Ali, by hiding in large jars inside a cave. They (6)_____ discovered by a slave girl, (7)_____, who saves Ali Baba by (8)_____ boiling oil on the thieves in the jars. The tales (9)_____ describe clever or lucky heroes like Ali Baba or Sindbad the Sailor (10)_____ to escape all the dangers which they have to face, while acquiring both the beautiful heroine and immense wealth.

- (1)   known, entitled, recognised
- (2)   has, have, had
- (3)   so, same, such
- (4)   particularly, purely, perfectly
- (5)   make, cause, plan
- (6)   are, were, will be
- (7)   therefore, however, though
- (8)   running, putting, pouring
- (9)   habitually, usually, specially
- (10) succeeding, trying, managing

4.7 Vocabulary: Negative prefixes

The following prefixes are used in English to make an adjective negative:

1   The prefix *un-* is used with the ordinary everyday words of English, and means 'not':

happy : unhappy   eatable : uneatable
friendly : unfriendly   cooked : uncooked

2   The prefix *in-* is used with many words of Latin origin, and also means 'not':

secure : insecure   complete : incomplete
formal : informal   frequent : infrequent

The prefix *in-* may, however, alter its sound and spelling in four ways:

in + l = ill-   legal : illegal
in + m = imm-   modest : immodest
in + p = imp-   possible : impossible
in + r = irr-   regular : irregular

Additionally, not all adjectives of Latin origin take *in-*. Some take *un-*, and these must simply be learned as you meet them:

necessary : unnecessary   satisfactory : unsatisfactory
real : unreal   stable : unstable

3   The prefix *non-* is sometimes in contrast with the other two:

scientific : non-scientific (= not at all scientific)
: unscientific   (= not good enough to be called
scientific)

Now study the example below and complete the sentences.

Example   He behaved in a rather _____ way towards her.   **friendly**
   ▷   He behaved in a rather unfriendly way towards her.

a.   Cats are more _____than dogs.   **dependent**

b.   I think it is very _____ that he has been to China.   **probable**

c.   That is a pretty _____ story.   **interesting**

d.   He is a doctor but he has been engaged on _____ work for years.   **medical**

e.   They went away and left the house _____.   **guarded**

f. She is the most _____ person I ever met.   **forgettable**

g. The ship was left _____ by the ice.   **damaged**

h. These supplies are _____ for the journey.   **sufficient**

i. It is quite _____ to try and do that work now.   **practical**

j. The figure was completely _____ against the   **visible**
    bright light.

4.8 Controlled composition: 'The Discontented Frogs'

Create a passage of several paragraphs from the material printed below. It is taken from *Aesop's Fables*.

1   there/be/time/ancient/Athens/when/people/be/unhappy/with/king/Peisistratos

2   he/not/do/very/much/and/they/consequently/want/better/more/active/sort/king

3   traveller/call/Aesop/tell/they/that/there/be/once/community/frog/that/feel/same/way

4   frog/be/just/unhappy/as/Athenian/

5   at/first/they/be/in/even/worse/situation/because/they/have/no/king/at/all

6   they/therefore/ask/great/god/Zeus/give/they/one

7   Zeus/think/about/it/and/say/that/in/he/opinion/frog/be/stupid

8   they/be/better/off/without/king

9   in/order/please/they/however/he/throw/large/log/wood/into/pool/where/they/live/and/say/that/it/would/make/they/very/fine/king/indeed

10 King Log/make/great/splash/when/he/arrive

11 at/first/frog/be/frighten/of/their/new/ruler/and/hide/from/he

12 however/they/soon/get/used/he/and/see/that/he/only/make/one/big/splash

13 they/therefore/grow/bold/and/begin/jump/all/over/their/new/king/show/no/respect/at/all

14 their/opinion/great/god/Zeus/be/not/very/high/either

15 they/tell/he/take/this/useless/king/away/and/give/they/proper/king/with/some/life/in/he

16 Zeus/be/annoy/their/stupidity

17 their/demand/would/however/be/meet/for/he/send/they/tall/ hungry/sharp-eyed/stork

18 when/King Stork/arrive/he/make/no/splash/but/be/full/life

19 he/be/fond/frog/and/soon/he/be/full/they/too

4.9 Editing a text: 'The Powerful Pigs'

Below is a short description of the plot of the book *Animal Farm*, by George Orwell, a kind of modern Aesop. The description is not, however, quite good enough. It contains a number of spelling, punctuation and grammatical errors. Edit the passage.

There was once a farmer who did not do his work very well and was cruel to his animals. It is not surprising therefore, that the animals hated him and that they met secretly in order to plan a revolution. Pigs led the revolution and the other animals followed.

The animals chased the bad farmer out and set up a special new form of government where all the animal were to be equal, no one would to walk on two legs like the farmer and no one would live in the frightening farmhouse.

Things went quite well for a time after that, the pigs were the cleverest animals on farm and were good leader They told the other animals what to do and began to enjoy to give orders. They even train the young dogs as a kind of police force. to make sure that the rest of the animals did exactly as they were ordered. Some pigs were not entirely happy about this new way of doing things however. They had originally believed strongly in a true and equal revolution. These pigs were not left in peace, they were chased out like the farmer, and some were even killed. Meanwhile the other pig moved into the farmhouse which was clearly the best place for leaders to live. Life for most of the animals was not much better now than it been before the revolution – but at least the new masters did not walk on two legs. In fact the animals worked harder than ever and, though life was better for the pigs it was not better for the majority of the inhabitants of Animal Farm. The pigs had an explanation for this, however. They agreed that all animals were equal, but they insist that some animals were more equal than others.

UNIT 5   Revision

5.1   Comprehension: 'I Saw It Happen'

Study the text and answer the questions that follow.

A road accident can turn a very ordinary day into a nightmare. The automobile is a wonderful machine in so many ways, but it can also be the cause of all kinds of pain, whether simply physical or emotional and mental. If people drive properly, then their cars have a kind of social magic about them, making possible a variety of   5
things that could not otherwise be done. But when people drive badly . . .

There was a nasty accident in our town not long ago, and I saw it happen.

I was standing near some roadworks, not doing anything special   10
– just watching the men at work. It was not far from the new motorway that runs past the town. It was an old road that used to be very busy – and dangerous – before the motorway was built.

Nowadays, the new 'super-highway' takes the bulk of the traffic
and the old road is pretty quiet, although traffic does often come off   15
the motorway into the town faster than it should.

Anyway, the men were repairing part of the road and there were
signs up for at least 200 metres, telling everybody that the road was
narrower than usual. Most of the drivers in both directions saw the
signs and slowed down. Then three cars came along close together,   20
the third one moving at a terrific speed. The first one passed the
roadworks and signalled to turn right. Meanwhile, the third car
came flying past the second one. The second car stopped. I think the
driver knew something was going to happen.

It did.   25

The third car had no chance of stopping. Its driver braked and
pulled over to miss the first car – and went straight off the road.

There were four people in that car: a man, two women and a
child. The child was a boy of nine. I read later that they were going
shopping – just shopping, nothing more urgent than that. The   30
driver was badly injured. The little boy was injured too. Both the
women were killed instantly. One of them was the driver's wife and
the other was the mother of the little boy. They never got to the
shops.

1   Are the following statements true (T) or false (F), in terms of the
passage? If a statement is false, say why.

a. ☐ Cars, properly driven, make many things possible that
could not be done otherwise.

b. ☐ Pain can be more than just physical.

c. ☐ The accident happened on a new fast road.

d. ☐ Most of the traffic nowadays goes on the motorway past
the town.

e. ☐ The second car was travelling far too fast.

f. ☐ The third car could not avoid hitting the first car.

g. ☐ The real trouble began when the third car passed the second
car.

h. ☐ The driver of the third car could not keep his vehicle on the
road.

i. ☐ The people in the second car were badly injured.

j. ☐ The driver of the third car was the little boy's father.

2   Can you find the following in the passage?

    a.   a general statement of fact in the form of a simple sentence

    b.   a general statement of fact in the form of a compound sentence

    c.   an example of a definite article being used with a singular noun to indicate a type (like *the cat*)

    d.   a general statement of fact in the form of a conditional sentence

    e.   the point at which the passage changes from general to particular

    f.   two uses of a participial phrase (with present participles) instead of a relative clause beginning with *that* or *which*

    g.   a specially quoted word

    h.   two paragraphs each containing only one sentence

    i.   three examples of a single dash used for dramatic effect

    j.   a parenthetical addition to a sentence

    k.   the point at which the general background description of the accident changes to the particular events

    l.   two uses of the relative pronoun *that* coming more or less one after the other

    m.   a concessional clause

    n.   a sentence with the relative pronoun (*that* or *which*) omitted

    o.   two examples of very short simple sentences used for dramatic effect

5.2   Spelling: A test

Ask a friend to test you with the following words:

swimmer	accommodation	achievement
occurred	easiest	occasional
exciting	lazily	seize
knowledge	necessarily	successfully
developing	friendlier	receiver
preferred	dying	embarrass
conscious	tried	foreign
journeyed	written	committee
omission	description	thief
correspondence	icy	believing

5.3 Spelling and organization: Alphabetic order

Below is a list of many of the technical words used in this course. Re-arrange these words in strict alphabetic order.

consequence	reference	reason
double	comma	definite
vocabulary	comprehension	tense
conditional	edit	structure
grammar	spelling	vocal
control	analysis	consonant
model	style	composition
dialogue	sentence	passage
comparison	result	suffix
parenthetical	participle	participial
relative	analytical	relation
communication	grammatical	communicate
voice	synthesis	conjunction
singular	plural	single
vowel	connection	period
speech	article	punctuation
synthetic	pronoun	text
test	phrase	parenthesis
quotation	prefix	positive
unit	compare	concession

5.4 Grammar: Conjunctions and relative pronouns

Below is a short list of the conjunctions and relative pronouns used so far in this course. Below that is a passage with appropriate blanks. Put the right connecting word in each blank. Some words need to be used more than once, and some are not needed at all.

although	but	or	what	which
and	how	so	when	while
because	if	that	where	who

(1)_____ it does not happen very often, animals do sometimes escape from zoos. (2)_____ you do not believe me, then read on,

(3)_____ this is a true story (4)_____ happened to a veterinarian called Oliver Graham-Jones. It occurred on a day (5)_____ the zoological gardens (6)_____ he worked were crowded with people, (7)_____ the escaping animals were only a short distance from the visitors.

The vet was involved in the matter (8)_____ he stopped to have a word with the men (9)_____ were looking after the Lion House. At the time (10)_____ it all happened they were standing near the passage (11)_____ divided the lions' sleeping area from the front cages (12)_____ the public could see them. There were several bridges over this passage, bridges (13)_____ allowed the great cats to move freely from their dens to their cages. The bridges were supposed to be strong, (14)_____ had iron bars and wooden floors. (15)_____ the Lion House was one of the biggest animal houses in the zoo, it was an old building, with dark shadowy corners, (16) _____ had perhaps not been well enough maintained.

Graham-Jones and the keepers were talking and he was standing with his back to the passageway itself (17)_____ one of the men gave a sudden shout of horror and concern. The vet turned round, to see (18)_____ was wrong. He saw (19)_____ part of the floor of one of the bridges had collapsed into the passageway. Pieces of wood were falling, and with them came a lion and a lioness! They were both very surprised animals indeed (20)_____ they hit the floor.

to be continued

5.5 Grammar: Articles

The account of Graham-Jones's adventure with the lions is continued below. This time, however, the blanks in the passage relate to possible missing definite and indefinite articles. Insert articles where necessary, putting an 'X' where in your opinion no article is needed.

For (1)_____ moment the men could not believe (2)_____ evidence of their own eyes. Then (3)_____ full danger of (4)_____ situation struck them. In (5)_____ matter of seconds (6)____ two big cats would be out in (7)_____ open, out among (8)_____ happy visitors.

What did one do in (9)_____ situation like that?

(10)_____ vet admitted later that he just did not know what to do. He just stood there. But one of (11)_____ keepers acted. He ran along (12)_____ passageway, and (13)_____ luck seemed to be with him.

'Get back!' he shouted at (14)_____ bewildered beasts. 'You two cats just get back into your den!'

(15)_____ lions are unpredictable creatures. Now, they just stood and stared at the man, tails twitching, looking slightly worried.

'Get back! You heard what I said! Get back to your den!'

(16)_____ male began to swish his tail, while (17)_____ female crouched down. Then to (18)_____ surprise of everyone there, (19)_____ tension went out of them, and one behind (20)_____ other they jumped back on to the bridge. (21)_____ moments later, they were safely back in their den.

(22)_____ emergencies like that can be (23)_____ terrible things – for all concerned. (24)_____ public never knew how narrowly they had escaped, and Graham-Jones never knew who was more worried at the time: (25)_____ lions or him.

5.6 Controlled composition: 'Gulliver's Travels'

Gulliver's Travels by Jonathan Swift first appeared in the year 1726. It is a classic of the English language and tells the strange story of the travels of Lemuel Gulliver. The material below provides an outline of some of the things that can be found in the book, and makes comments upon them. Convert it into a clear grammatical passage.

1   book/call/Gulliver/travel/be/in/many/way/similar/to/ thousand/one/night/and/Aesop/fable/because/it/use/ strange/situation/in/faraway/land/and/also/make/ humorous/comment/on/human/nature

2   it/be/therefore/fantasy/with/practical/purpose

3   essential/the/book/describe/what/happen/Gulliver/whenever/ he/go/long/sea/voyage

4   on/first/occasion/his/ship/be/wreck/and/he/find/himself/ Lilliput/land/little/people

5   late/he/go/by/accident/land/giant/call/Brobdingnag

6   on/still/another/occasion/he/have/adventure/land/talk/horses

7 in/fact/all/this/little/people/giant/horses/represent/human/
being

8 author/Jonathan Swift/like/write/about/people/politics/
society/and/suggest/from/certain/point/view/important/
problems/in/country/might/appear/very/small/
unimportant

9 Swift/also/mean/some/people/have/small/mind/and/need/
realize/just/how/insignificant/they/be/in/universe

10 he/suggest/some/horse/mind/be/perhaps/good/than/some/
people/or/at/least/it/be/interesting/hear/intelligent/
speech/come/from/horse

11 although/today/Gulliver/travel/be/read/mainly/for/sake/of/
stories/originally/Swift/write/it/in/order/shock/people/
and/in/this/he/succeed

UNIT 6

6.1 Comprehension and composition model: 'The Marriage Market'

Early-nineteenth-century engraving showing the style of clothes and dance typical of the period when *Pride and Prejudice* was written.

Here is a short passage about parents, daughters and marriage. It is adapted from the beginning of Jane Austen's novel, *Pride and Prejudice*, first published in 1813. Note how it is laid out on the page, and read it twice.

> Everyone knows, says Jane Austen, that an unmarried man with money needs a wife. Mrs Bennet certainly knew this, and also knew that just such a young man had arrived in the neighbourhood. In fact, he had rented nearby Netherfield Park. His name was Bingley, and he was from the north. 5

Mrs Bennet's interest in Mr Bingley was simple. She had five unmarried daughters. It was only reasonable to assume that, if he had a suitable opportunity, he would fall in love with one of them. Which of them was not really important.

For this reason, therefore, she spoke to her husband about the   10
interesting newcomer, because, after all, she could not make any plans until Mr Bennet had called on the unsuspecting Mr Bingley. When that was done, she could invite him to their home, where the young ladies could be best displayed.

'And so, my dear, you must go and see him.'   15

'I had no plan to do so,' said Mr Bennet.

'But you must. Consider your daughters. He has a great deal of money, so I hear, and it would be a perfectly wonderful match for one of them.'

'Perhaps you could just write a list of the good qualities of each   20
girl and I could send it to him.'

'I will do nothing of the kind!'

'Well then, Elizabeth is the best.'

'You *always* prefer Elizabeth.'

'I don't. They are just silly and ignorant girls like all other girls.   25
Elizabeth is a little brighter, that's all.'

'You're just trying to annoy me. It will be very bad for us if you don't call on him.'

'You think so? There will be plenty more like him, my dear.'

'That won't help us if you never visit any of them!'   30

Mr Bennet sighed. Perhaps he sympathized with the young man. Perhaps he was thinking of all the other local mothers urging all the other local fathers to call instantly on the poor gentleman from the north. He agreed, however, to do as she asked, both because his wife was a determined woman and because he did indeed have five   35
unmarried daughters on his hands.

Below are some statements relating to the passage. Some are true (T) in terms of the passage, while others are false (F). Mark them appropriately, and if a statement is false, say why.

a. ☐ Mrs Bennet knew that the young man at Netherfield Park wanted a wife.

b. ☐ Mr Bingley had bought the house called Netherfield Park.

c. ☐ She intended to invite the young man to her home immediately, in order to meet her girls.

d. ☐ Mr Bennet had been planning to call on Mr Bingley.

e. ☐ He thought that the other girls were a little slower than Elizabeth.

f. ☐ He thought that Mr Bingley was only one of many unmarried men with money.

g. ☐ Mr Bennet definitely sympathized with Mr Bingley.

h. ☐ Mr Bennet was really just like his wife. He wanted to see all his daughters safely married.

6.2 Spelling: Commonly misspelt words

Below is a list of twenty-four words that are often misspelled because they contain double letters. Memorize how they look, getting a friend to test you.

accidentally	career	necessary	professor
accommodation	committee	occasionally	recommend
address	correspondence	occurred	referred
all right	embarrass	occurrence	succeed
assassin	goddess	possession	success
beginning	immediately	preferred	successfully

6.3 Grammar: Direct and indirect speech

Spoken words can be expressed in writing in two ways:

1 in *direct speech*, using special punctuation and layout:

'He has a great deal of money,' she said.

2 in *indirect* or *reported speech*, which is much more like normal writing:

She said that he had a great deal of money.

Notice the change of tense from *has* to *had*. This is typical of the change from direct to indirect speech. The table below gives some examples of expressions changing in this way:

Direct speech	Indirect speech
has	had
is	was
comes	came
can	could
will	would
tomorrow	the next day
yesterday	the day before

76

Now study the examples and change the sentences in the same way.

Example 1 'Mr Bingley has a great deal of money,' said Mrs Bennet.
or
Mrs Bennet said: 'Mr Bingley has a great deal of money.'

▷ Mrs Bennet said that Mr Bingley had a great deal of money.
or (less formally)
Mrs Bennet said Mr Bingley had a great deal of money.

Example 2 'You are just trying to annoy me,' she said.
or
She said: 'You are just trying to annoy me.'

▷ She said that he was just trying to annoy her.
or (less formally)
She said he was just trying to annoy her.

a. 'A new young man has just come to Netherfield Park,' said Mrs Bennet.
b. 'His name is Bingley and he comes from the north,' she added.
c. 'You should call him tomorrow,' she suggested.
d. 'I have no plan to do so,' said Mr Bennet, cautiously.
e. 'He will make a wonderful match for one of the girls,' she said, firmly.
f. He suggested: 'You should make a list of the good qualities of each girl and I can send it to the young man.'
g. She said angrily, 'I will do nothing of the kind!'
h. 'Elizabeth is the best,' said her husband.
i. 'You always prefer Elizabeth,' she answered.
j. 'I don't,' he replied with a smile.

6.4 Punctuation:
Dialogue, quotation and reference

Writers have a variety of reasons for quoting what other people have said or written. They also need from time to time to make some word, phrase or sentence 'stand out' from the rest. For these purpose *quotation marks* (also known as *speech marks* and *inverted commas*) are used. Here are some uses of quotation marks that have already appeared in this course;

1   In the passage on *Cats* (lines 9–10):

   A male cat gets a special name to show that he is not a female. He is a 'tomcat'.

   It is perfectly possible not to use quotation marks here, but they serve clearly to show that the writer is introducing a special new word.

2   In the passage on *The Warship* (lines 17–19):

   She drove herself onward and downward into the rolling waters, 'to the black floor of the Arctic', her great engines still turning – and took every man with her.

   Here the quotation marks are essential, because the writer is directly quoting some words from the original novel by Alistair Maclean.

3   In the passage called *The Marriage Market* (lines 15 onward):

   'And so, my dear, you must go and see him.'

   'I had no plan to do so,' said Mr Bennet.

   This is the kind of conversational material that we find in novels, newspapers, magazines and so on. It follows a complex set of rules which need a great deal of time, practice and skill to use well.

Essentially, there are two tendencies in the use of quotation marks: the traditional and the modern. The traditional style uses double marks (the true 'inverted commas' often taught to children as 66 and 99), whereas the modern style uses single marks:

Traditional   "Come in," she said.
Modern   'Come in,' she said.

In the table opposite you will see the arrangements made for those occasions when speech occurs inside speech, or a quotation inside a quotation:

Traditional   "He said 'Get out!'" she sobbed.
(" '   ' ")

Modern   'He said "Get out!"' she sobbed.
(' "   " ')

Unless you intend to become a professional writer of stories and articles, you should not spend too much time on this kind of thing – although it is important to have a good basic knowledge of how it is done. The following points may help in this:

1   You can make a word, phrase or sentence stand out in your writing by various means. You could put the whole thing in quotation marks, or you could underline it, or you could use capital letters. All of these are acceptable, but should be done with care. Writers who are very eager to influence people may well over-use all of these techniques. The result is a page of print or writing which is too agitated. It shouts at the reader.

2   If you are writing something which will definitely be published or printed, then anything that is underlined will automatically be converted by the printer into italic letters – unless you indicate otherwise. Take care, therefore, with what you underline.

3   Putting a single word in quotation marks suggests that in some way it is special or unusual: it is being quoted, or it is a metaphor, or slang, a technical term, a dialect word, a child's word, a foreign word, or something of the kind.

4   The titles of books, films, etc, are usually underlined in writing and typing and in italics in print. The titles of chapters or articles inside books, etc, are usually placed between quotation marks, as follows:

> In the course entitled *The Written Word*, the passage in Unit 1 is called 'Cats' and the passage in Unit 5 is called 'The Marriage Market'.

Note that in a case like this the period comes after the last quotation mark, not before it. In conversation, the period comes before the last quotation mark:

> She said: 'I hope he'll come.'

5   Optionally, the names of plays, films, ships, works of art, etc, can be underlined, italicized or put between quotation marks. The important thing is to choose one of these methods and stick to it throughout a piece of writing. Never mix techniques. Different techniques in the same piece of writing mean (or *should* mean) different intentions.

6   A writer should also choose which of the two kinds of quotation marks to use – single or double – and then stick to that style. One should not have, for example, single marks for words and phrases, then double marks for conversation. The same kind of marks should be used throughout.

Now punctuate the three passages below:

Passage 1

well my dear did you call on mr bingley asked mrs bennet excitedly yes I did he replied smiling what happened well you may be glad to know that we shall be seeing this young gentleman quite soon when where what on earth do you mean mr bennet laughed pleased at his wifes response it is simple my dear he answered he has been invited to the ball and has agreed to go he will therefore have every opportunity not only to see but also to dance with every one of our daughters if he has a mind to do so

Passage 2

pride and prejudice is probably the most famous of jane austens six novels about life love and marriage among the middle classes of early 19th century england the other novels are sense and sensibility emma mansfield park persuasion and northanger abbey her style of writing mixes realism with romance in a way that was quite revolutionary at the time she knew the society that she described and took care not to move beyond it into subjects and places of which she had no personal knowledge and experience it was unusual at that time for **quote** well bred **end quote** ladies to write publish and earn money from books and she therefore did not allow her name to appear on any of her books sir walter scott in the quarterly review of march 1816 praised this **quote** nameless author **end quote** as a master of **quote** the modern novel **end quote** jane austen died the following year at the age of 42 and it was only then that her authorship of the novels was revealed to the public by her brother henry she was indeed as scott suggested a master of her craft using ordinary everyday people and events in order to deal with the rich tragedy and comedy of human life

Passage 3

maria knew that he was coming she put on her flowered dress with bows on the sleeves combed her shiny black hair carefully and having got ready earlier than usual went every now and again to the window and looked up the road at last abel came he came on a bicycle which he put beside the gate is maria at home he asked me

nervously sure I said I ran inside to get her although she already
knew very well that he was there it was all part of the game I didnt
expect to see you she lied when she came out I was getting dressed
to go out but the way she smiled told abel something different
much later I saw maria and abel down by the river I was with ruth
and we hid among the bushes and watched with interest abel took
maria in his arms gently and gave her her first kiss you cant call
that a kiss at all said ruth but she had hardly said this when abel
kissed maria again and this time for so long that I wondered how
they could hold their breath thats what you can really call a kiss
said ruth with respect

6.5 Grammar and punctuation: Ellipsis

The term 'ellipsis' refers to the omission of parts of sentences, usually
because they are not really needed, or in ordinary writing to produce
a special effect. Ellipsis is very common in English writing, and a
knowledge of how it operates can help improve one's style.

Basically, ellipsis depends upon context. If the context is clear,
then one can shorten certain sentences quite a lot. It is dangerous,
however, to be too elliptical, because this can sometimes interfere
with the reader's ability to understand the text. The following five
sentences show just how far a statement can be reduced (under
certain circumstances) and still make sense:

I do not prefer Elizabeth to the other girls.
I do not prefer Elizabeth to the others.
I do not prefer Elizabeth.
I do not.
I don't.

The first sentence is complete and clear. The second can only be
used successfully if the reader is already aware that 'others' means
'other girls'. The third can only be used successfully if the reader is
already aware of the others to whom Elizabeth is being compared,
and so on. The fifth sentence, of course, is a special kind of informal
reduction, usually representing how we speak.

Sometimes a writer wants to omit something deliberately, to
achieve a special effect. The commonest effect of all is the unfinished
statement, where the reader must imagine the rest:

'Can I help you?'

'Well . . .'

'I would be happy to help you.'

'Well, perhaps, if you could -um- lend me some money, then . . .'

The three points (. . .) are the usual method of showing this second kind of ellipsis, but occasionally a dash is used instead. In expressions like *don't*, *can't*, *I'll* and so on, the apostrophe (') of course serves to mark the omission. Ellipses of this kind tend to occur in representations of speech or in informal writing. Usually, informal and dramatic forms of ellipsis are avoided in writing formal reports, essays and descriptions.

Now use the examples to help you develop the art of ellipsis.

Example 1   I did not know that he had done it all himself.

▷   I didn't know he'd done it all himself.

In this example, the reduced sentence is more informal than the original. In the ten sentences that follow some will become informal when reduced. Mark them (IR). Others will have essentially the same meaning and level of style. Mark them (SR).

a. ☐ I like the people, I like the town and I like the houses.

b. ☐ Who do you think he had seen?

c. ☐ Women usually like shopping, but men do not usually like shopping.

d. ☐ I will go if you will go.

e. ☐ He went with her in order to get the money.

f. ☐ The men who were guarding the building fell asleep one by one.

g. ☐ Shahriyar, who was King of Persia, disliked women.

h. ☐ He is certainly the man whom we met yesterday.

i. ☐ She does not have to tell them that they have won.

j. ☐ He found the second story just as interesting as the first story had been.

Example 2   *Pride and Prejudice* is a novel written by Jane Austen and it begins with a conversation between Mr and Mrs Bennet.

▷   *Pride and Prejudice*, written by Jane Austen, begins with a conversation between Mr and Mrs Bennet.

In this elliptical reduction a neater style emerges, and it is assumed – safely enough – that everyone knows that the book is a novel. Perform the same kind of reduction on the sentences below.

k. *HMS Ulysses* is a book written by Alistair Maclean which describes the fate of a warship in Arctic waters.

l. The Frogs, who were eager to have an active and interesting king, asked the great god Zeus for his help.

m. *The Arabian Nights* is a collection of stories from the East and is set in ancient Iran.

n. The sailors, who were afraid in case *The Northern Queen* would be trapped in the ice, sent urgent radio messages for help.

o. *Aesop's Fables* is an ancient Greek collection of tales which uses insect and animal characters to describe human nature.

p. This temple was built by the Romans and is a perfect example of classical architecture.

q. *Animal Farm*, written by George Orwell, is a book with a social and political purpose.

r. The fine old house was built by his family in the 18th century and has been their home ever since.

6.6 Grammar: Expressing possibilities

There are many ways in which possibilities can be expressed in English. The most obvious way is to use the adjective *possible*, while the simplest way is to use the modal verbs *may* and *might*. Other ways, however, include using *perhaps* and *maybe*. Seven separate forms are shown in the following table:

1 *It is possible that* he will come tomorrow.	a formal and logical statement
2 *It's possible* he'll come tomorrow.	the same, informally
3 He *may* come tomorrow.	shorter and probably commoner than 1 and 2
4 He *might* come tomorrow.	much the same as 3, but suggesting greater doubt
5 *Perhaps* he will / he'll come tomorrow.	a common spoken and written alternative to 3
6 *Maybe* he will / he'll come tomorrow.	an informal alternative to 3, common in general conversation
7 *Perhaps* he *may* / *might* come tomorrow.	a less common alternative, more emphatic than the others

83

Below are five sentences. Each of these sentences represents one of the types in the table. Re-express each in the six other possible ways.

a.   It is possible that he will talk to Mr Bingley.

b.   Elizabeth may need your help.

c.   They might not see Mr Bennet after all.

d.   Perhaps they will leave soon.

e.   Maybe I'll go there next week.

Possibility may also be related to ability. In the next table, the relationship between *may/might*, *be able* and *can/could* is shown:

1 *It is possible that* he will be able to help you.	a formal and logical statement
2 *It's possible* he'll be able to help you.	the same informally
3 He $\frac{may}{might}$ be able to help you.	common everyday usage
4 *Perhaps* he $\frac{is\ able}{will\ be\ able}$ to help you.	a fairly common spoken and written alternative to 3
5 *Perhaps* he can help you.	shorter and probably commoner than 4
6 *Perhaps* he could help you	less direct and expressing more doubt than 5

7   *Maybe* he'll be able to help you.
        he can help you.
        he could help you.
	informal alternatives, common in general conversation

8 *Perhaps* he $\frac{may}{might}$ be able to help you.	a less common alternative, more emphatic than the others

Note   Take care not to confuse the adverbial form *maybe* with the verb forms *may be* (as in 'He may be coming').

Below are five more sentences. Each represents one of the types in the table. Re-express each in the seven other forms.

f.   Mr Bingley may be able to come.

g.   Perhaps you will be able to find Elizabeth.

h.   Maybe we can all go there together.

i.   Mrs Bennet may not be able to find husbands for all her daughters.

j.   They might not be able to go the ball after all.

The words *whether* and *if* are both often used to express alternative possibilities, one positive, the other negative. Use the examples given below to re-express the sentences that follow them in the same ways.

Examples   He may come.   He may not (come).   I do not know.
Perhaps he will come.   Perhaps not.   I do not know.
Maybe he'll come.   Maybe he won't.   I don't know.

▷   { I do not know *whether/if* he will come or not.   **formal**
     { I don't know *whether/if* he'll come or not.   **informal**

k.   Mr Bingley may have a lot of money. He may not. I do not know.

l.   He may talk to us at the ball. He may not. We do not know.

m.   Perhaps they can come. Perhaps they cannot. He is not sure.

n.   Maybe he went. Maybe he didn't. Who knows?

o.   Perhaps she will find it. Perhaps not. They are not at all sure.

6.7 Vocabulary: Forming words

Many words in English have their origins in the Latin and Greek languages. Other words are usually formed from them in ways that also originate in Latin and Greek. Here are two such ways:

1   Certain nouns of Latin origin (especially those ending in *-ion*, *-ic(s)* and *-ure*) form an adjective by adding *-al* and an adverb by adding *-ally*:

addition : additional : additionally
music : musical : musically
ethics : ethical : ethically
nature : natural : naturally

2   Certain nouns of Greek origin form an adjective by adding *-ic* (with the stress in the adjective falling on the syllable before the *-ic*), and an adverb by adding *-ically*:

atom : atomic : atomically
athlete : athletic : athletically

Some belong to special groups which require the addition of extra elements:

idiom : idiomatic : idiomatically
drama : dramatic : dramatically
sympathy : sympathetic : sympathetically

Additionally, some words share patterns that are mixed Latin and Greek, and sometimes this means that two adjectives can be formed from one noun, each with a slightly different meaning (that you can find in a good dictionary), but sharing the same adverb:

economy : economic/economical : economically
history : historic/historical : historically
geography : geographic/geographical : geographically

Now study the example below and complete the sentences. You may need an adjective or an adverb, and in some cases you may also need a negative prefix (as in Section 4.7).

Example	I did not like it because it seemed very _____ to me.	**nature**
▷	I did not like it because it seemed very unnatural to me.	
a.	It was an exciting and _____ tale about sailors, ships and ice.	**drama**
b.	The material was not _____ interesting because we could never sell it at a profit.	**commerce**
c.	She did not help him because when she needed help he had been rather _____ towards her.	**sympathy**
d.	It is a fine old _____ building and we are proud to have it in our city.	**history**
e.	She is always falling in love, but he is an _____ kind of person.	**romance**
f.	The party is _____, so you don't need to dress up for it.	**form**
g.	He is not well known outside the country, but _____ he is very well known indeed.	**nation**
h.	She speaks Portuguese well, but she is not yet fluent _____.	**idiom**
i.	They like sports and play a very _____ game of tennis.	**energy**
j.	The _____ aspect of life in India is very rich and complex.	**culture**

k.	It is a poor country and, _____ speaking, is underdeveloped.	**industry**
l.	When an adult learns a foreign language, it is probably a good idea to learn its grammar in a _____ way.	**system**
m.	She spoke very _____ about her various beliefs, making it clear that she did not expect other people to agree with her.	**dogma**
n.	Can I speak to you _____ about a rather personal matter?	**confidence**
o.	Although they were very interested in the question of love and marriage, they tried to discuss it in a friendly but _____ manner.	**person**
p.	When things are going well, it is probably _____ to go out and deliberately cause trouble.	**reason** (= **ration-**)
q.	It is completely _____ to do that and you could go to prison if you were caught.	**law** (= **leg-**)

6.8 Controlled composition: 'Coming to See the Girl'

The passage adapted from Jane Austen said something about arranging marriages in early 19th-century England. You can now create a passage about arranging marriages in present-day India.

1   in/India/marriage/be/usual/<u>arrange</u>/parent

2   most/young/people/<u>accept</u>/this/state/affairs/quite/happy/and/ <u>assume</u>/that/their/parent/<u>can</u>/<u>make</u>/good/choice/their/ behalf

3   sometimes/however/girl/boy/<u>do</u>/not/<u>like</u>/idea/arranged/ marriage

4   shantha/<u>be</u>/like/that

5   she/<u>feel</u>/she/<u>be</u>/modern/girl/and/not/subject/bargaining/ between/family

6   she/therefore/<u>hope</u>/that/her/parent/<u>would</u>/not/start/<u>look</u>/for/ husband/for/she

7   one/day/however/shantha/<u>come</u>/home/college/and/<u>see</u>/mango leaves/<u>hang</u>/over/front/door

8   these leaves/be/sign/welcome/people/come/see/girl

9   oh/no/she/think/what/shall/I/do

10   meanwhile/Shantha/mother/think/daughter/would/soon/leave/home/in/order/start/own/life

11   her/mother/think/things/buy/wedding/and/Shantha/new/home

12   she/think/boy/parent/would/ask/if/Shantha/have/bank/account/make/young/couple/life/more/comfortable

13   boy/be/tall/and/have/good/job

14   his/parent/would/ask/things/like/bank/account/because/be/easy/find/wife/such/boy

15   Shantha/meanwhile/think/she/be/not/something/bargain/about/but/be/also/frightened/case/visit/prove/unsuccessful

16   doorbell/ring/house/sudden/seem/full/people/talk/ask/question

17   people/ask/whether/daughter/have/return/yet/college

18   Shantha/mother/say/yes/I'll/go/get/she

19   Shantha/who/wait/say/mother/am/I/all/right

20   her/mother/smile/and/say/reassuring/I/know/you/be/just/perfect

UNIT 7

7.1 Comprehension and composition model: Football

Photograph 'Wesley Fesler kicks a rugby football' taken by Dr. Harold Edgerton, Cambridge Ma. USA.

Here is a short passage describing the history of the game called football. Read it twice, noting how the stages in the history of the game are developed, paragraph by paragraph.

Football is a very old game. The ancient Romans, Chinese and Mexicans all played games where men kicked a ball. For the Romans it was a war game, in which two teams of soldiers would use whatever force was necessary to get the ball across either of two defended lines. The Roman Empire has long since vanished, but the violent pastime of the legionaries has continued – and can still be quite violent!

5

In the Middle Ages, some kind of 'football' was popular in Italy, France, England and Scotland, but it was such a dangerous game that kings actually banned it, and for 300 years it suffered greatly from official disapproval. Nevertheless, in 1613, King James VI of Scotland and I of England permitted himself to be entertained in an English village with 'music and a football match', and, a few years later, the English dictator Oliver Cromwell played football when he was at university.

10

15

By the end of the 18th century, however, the game was in real danger of dying out in Western Europe. Curiously enough, it was the English 'public' school that saved it from extinction. The rich young men at these schools (which were in fact private rather than public) had nowhere to hunt, fish, ride or otherwise use up their energies; all they could do outside school hours was kick a ball in the schools' open spaces. They played the game that they had often seen played on village greens, the game that kings had banned, and each school slowly began to evolve its own special style and rules.

20

By the time of Queen Victoria, enthusiastic 17-year-old boys were writing out rules for what had once been no more than violent military or village fun. They also took the game with them to the universities, where they needed other rules, so that people who had played very different kinds of football at school could play together successfully at university. This was how the Football Association came into being. One public school, however, refused to co-operate, its delegates objecting to the new universal game. This school – Rugby – left the new association, to play its own game with its own oval-shaped ball that could be carried as well as kicked. In this way the 'soccer' of the association and the 'rugger' of Rugby were born and went their separate ways.

25

30

35

In 1863, the Football Association approved a game that outlawed carrying and kept the ball at men's feet. The game still had a long way to go, however, before it would be the soccer watched by millions around the world on television during the World Cup. Whole teams would rush back and forward on the field with the ball kept close at their feet; there were no passes or long kicks, and some of the rules used in those days were still nearer rugby than soccer. By the early 1870s, however, the fast exciting and open game of modern Association football was beginning to appear. The goal became standard, with a hard crossbar instead of a long piece of tape, and the goal-keeper was given his own personal set of rules. In the process, soccer changed irrevocably from a gentleman's weekend exercise to the greatest spectator sport in the history of the human race.

40

45

50

Below are some statements relating to the passage. Some are true (T) in terms of the passage, while others are false (F). Mark them appropriately, and if a statement is false, say why.

a. ☐ The ancient Mexicans played soccer.

b. ☐ Roman soldiers played football as a war game.

c. ☐ In 1613, King James banned the playing of football.

d. ☐ Rich schoolboys rescued the old village game of football from extinction.

e. ☐ In the early 19th century there were many different kinds of football.

f. ☐ When public schoolboys went to university and began to play football together the game became more and more standardized.

g. ☐ Even after the Football Association was formed the game was still not quite modern Association football.

h. ☐ In the game called rugby, players are permitted to handle the ball.

i. ☐ The modern games of soccer and rugger developed largely because Queen Victoria showed an enthusiastic interest in them.

j. ☐ There has never been a more popular spectator sport in the whole of human history than soccer.

7.2 Spelling:
Completing words

Below are ten sentences taken directly from the passage. In these sentences there are words with some letters missing. Each missing letter is indicated by means of a period (.). Complete each word properly spelled.

a. For the Romans it was a war game, in which two teams of sold . . rs would use whatever force was ne. . .s . ry to get the ball across either of two defended lines.

b. In the Middle Ages, some kind of 'football' was popul. . in Italy, France, England and Scotland, but it was such a dang . . . . . game that kings actually banned it.

c. Nevertheless, in 1613, King James VI of Scotland and I of England perm . . . . d himself to be entertained in an English village with 'music and a football match'.

d. By the end of the 18th century, however the game was in real danger of d . . ng out in Western Europe.

e. Cur . . . . . . enough, it was the English 'public' school that saved it from ex . . . . . ion.

f. The rich young men at these schools (which were in fact priv . . . rather than public) had n . . . . re to hunt, fish, ride or other . . . . use up their energies.

g. Each school slowly began to ev . . . . its own sp . . . . l st. le and rules.

h. By the time of Queen Victoria enth . . . . .tic 17-year-old boys were wr . . . . g out rules for what had once been no more than v . . . . nt mil . . . . y or village fun.

i. They also took the game with them to the universities, where they needed other rules, so that p . . . le who had played very d . . . . . . nt kinds of football at school could play together su . . e . . f . . . y at university.

j. By the early 1870s, however, the fast e . . . ting and open game of modern A . . . . . . tion football was beg . . . . ng to a . . . . r.

7.3 Grammar:
Uses of *would*

The modal verb *would* has a number of distinct uses in English, usually connected with or suggesting some kind of past action. In the table below, four such uses are shown:

Examples	Uses
1 I will do it if it is really necessary.	the expression of a condition in its
▷ I would do it if it was/were really necessary.	past form, suggesting that it is less immediate or likely
2 'They will come,' he said.	the expression of someone's speech
▷ He said that they would come.	or thought in its past form, as indirect information
3 The game has a long way to go before it is (**or** it will be) played everywhere.	the expression of the future in a past period of time
▷ The game had a long way to go before it was (**or** would be) played everywhere.	
4 They will play football on the village green whenever/if they can.	the expression of a habit, custom, desire, etc, in the past (sometimes
▷ They would play football on the village green whenever/if they could.	related to a stated or unstated condition)

Now mark each of the sentences that follow 1, 2, 3 or 4 in the squares provided, to indicate how *would* is used:

a. ☐ She told me that they would be late.

b. ☐ If pigs had wings they would fly.

c. ☐ On such occasions, the soldiers would use whatever force was necessary.

d. ☐ Would you believe it (if I told you)?

e. ☐ He knew that she would not help him.

f. ☐ The team still had a lot of games to win before they would be considered really good.

g. ☐ It would be good if you could play on Saturday with us.

h. ☐ He would just sit beside the fire, smoking his pipe and remembering old times.

i. ☐ They said they would not be leaving early.

j. ☐ Sometimes they would work hard and sometimes they would do nothing at all.

Note that in informal usage, *would* is usually reduced to *'d*, and *would not* becomes *wouldn't*:

He would like to help. ▷ He'd like to help.

He would not want that to happen. ▷ He wouldn't want that to happen.

Now, using the letters k–t, repeat the sentences above, reducing *would* to *'d*, and *would not* to *wouldn't*, where appropriate.

In addition to the points described above, *would* also has a special relationship with the expression *used to*, as shown in this table:

Examples	Uses
1 They played football on Saturday.	a simple past fact, the period of time involved *not* specified
2 They *used to* play football on Saturday (but not now).	a past fact, habit, custom, etc, extending over a period of time but definitely no longer occurring
3 They *would* play football on Saturday (if/when/ whenever possible).	a past fact, habit, custom, etc, suggesting a long period (and sometimes related to a stated or unstated condition)

Using the table, change each of the following sentences into the other two forms, noting how the meaning changes slightly:

u.   The whole teams would rush back and forward on the field.

v.   There used to be a lot of singing and dancing after the work was done.

w.   Years ago everybody went to town when there was a special holiday.

x.   During the war you would see people selling anything they had to get food.

y.   Kings used to ban the playing of football.

z.   He would sit beside the fire, smoking his pipe and remembering old times.

7.4 Grammar: Causes and effects

There are various ways of saying that a certain thing has happened after or as a result of some earlier thing. These ways often use the words *so* and *such*, as follows:

Examples	Uses
1 It was a violent game *and* they banned it.	two facts – cause and effect
2 It was a violent game, *so* they banned it.	an informal statement of consequence
3 It was *such* a violent game (*that*) they banned it.	a more formal statement of consequence
4 It was *so* violent a game *that* they banned it.	a more formal and emphatic statement of consequence
5 *So* violent a game was it *that* they banned it.	a very formal and rather old-fashioned statement of consequence
6 They banned it *because* it was such a violent game.	a simple statement of the reason for an action

Note that sentences 4 and 5 in the table only work for nouns in the singular form.

Now take each of the following sentences presenting two facts (cause and effect), and re-express them in all the other possible ways, considering carefully each difference in style:

a. It was a wonderful game and they really enjoyed it.

b. It was a boring game and they did not enjoy it.

c. It was an interesting sport and they liked watching it.

d. This is a strange story and it interests me very much.

e. It is a beautiful country and I want to go there.

f. He is a difficult man to talk to and I do not want to see him again.

7.5 Grammar and vocabulary: Causes and effects

Sometimes talking or writing about causes and effects can mean a change in an actual word (especially if that word is of Latin origin). Study the example below, then complete the sentences that follow, making the necessary changes in order to use the words printed on the right.

Example   The game was *violent*, so they banned it.   **violence**

▷ Because of
On account of ⎱ the game's *violence*, they banned it.
As a result of ⎰

or (more commonly)

Because of
On account of ⎱ its *violence*, they banned the game.
As a result of ⎰

a. She was beautiful and attracted many men.   **beauty**

b. They were excellent, so we sold many of them.   **excellence**

c. They are new, so we find the machines hard to use.   **newness**

d. She behaved badly, so they chose another candidate.   **bad behaviour**

e.   He is very able, so we can give him work any   **ability**
     time.

f.   She is kind, so children like her very much.   **kindness**

g.   These watches are accurate, so people buy a   **accuracy**
     lot of them.

h.   They are friendly, and most people like them.   **friendliness**

i.   She is unhappy, so nothing seems to go right   **unhappiness**
     for her.

j.   The country was invaded, so everybody had to   **invasion**
     fight.

7.6 Punctuation: The semi-colon

Look at these two sentences from the passage about football:

1   The rich young men at these schools (which   (lines 18–22)
    were in fact private rather than public) had
    nowhere to hunt, fish, ride or otherwise use up
    their energies; all they could do outside school
    hours was kick a ball in the schools' open
    spaces.

2   Whole teams would rush back and forward on   (lines 41–44)
    the field with the ball kept close at their feet;
    there were no passes or long kicks, and some of
    the rules used in those days were nearer rugby
    than soccer.

The semi-colon (;) serves as a kind of halfway mark between a period (.) and a comma (,). It is not surprising, therefore, that it is formed by putting one above the other. Each of the long sentences shown above could in fact be written as two sentences, with a period instead of a semi-colon, but writers sometimes prefer semi-colons in order to show a particularly close connection. It is, nevertheless, an option;

no one is obliged to use it. Sometimes several options are possible, as shown in the following table:

Examples	Usage
1 The ship sank. Eighteen lives were lost. It was a great tragedy.	clear, separate sentences, all equal
2 The ship sank; eighteen lives were lost. It was a great tragedy.	the first two sentences closely related as cause and effect, while the third sentence is a separate comment
3 The ship sank – eighteen lives were lost. It was a great tragedy.	the first two sentences dramatically related by means of a dash, to emphasize the cause and effect

The semi-colon is often used to show causes and effects as well as a variety of other logical relationships:

4   The work was inadequate; the project failed.

5   The work was inadequate; consequently, the project failed.

6   The work was inadequate; however, the project could still be saved.

7   He managed the business well; for example, he improved working conditions and still made a greater profit than ever before.

Punctuation work:
First stage

Punctuate the following passages, deciding (among other things) where to put one semi-colon per section:

a.   the rich young men had nowhere to fish hunt ride or otherwise use up their energies all they could do outside school hours was kick a ball in the schools open spaces it was out of such casual beginnings that the modern game of football emerged

b.   one public school however refused to co operate its delegates objecting to the new universal game rugby therefore left the new association it had its own plans the result of which was a very different kind of game

c.   since 1876 american football has been played by two teams of eleven players each it is however very different from soccer the ball is oval like a rugby ball and the players wear special padding and helmets to protect them from injuries although it is also played on an open field it looks completely different from both british games

d.   football developed rapidly in the 19th century by queen victorias time for example 17 year old schoolboys were engaged in writing out its rules taking the game with them to their universities where they needed further rule making so that people from different school backgrounds could play together this was how the world famous football association began

Punctuation work: Second stage

There is always a simple logical order in the sentences of a well-written passage. Below you will find eight sentences which make up a passage about Charles Alcock and the Football Association in England. These sentences are not, however, in their proper order, nor are they properly punctuated. Punctuate them fully, then re-arrange them to make sense.

A.   it was only in the 1950s that england returned to the international scene

B.   british people in europe and south america organized football clubs and local men enthusiastically joined them in a game which began to rediscover its international nature

C.   between 1870 and 1900 under the guidance of its remarkable secretary charles alcock the f a changed soccer from a gentlemans weekend pastime into a great sporting spectacle

D.   in 1904 a number of european associations asked england to help in organizing an international federation it is however a curious fact that she refused to do so and let world football develop on its own for many years

E.   in the 1880s he faced the hard work of creating the football league and established a world pattern for regular weekend competitions

F.   in 1871 alcock founded the f a challenge cup the first of the knockout competitions leading towards todays world cup

G.   mexicans chinese and italians among many other nations began once more to play the dangerous and exciting game that had once taken the place of war

H.   in the same year he took an english team to play in scotland and so created international football

7.7 Vocabulary: Nations and nationalities

In English we have a very wide range of different ways of forming the names of nationalities. These differences have arisen because of the various times in history when English-speaking peoples came in contact with other nations. There are, however, several major patterns for the formation of nationality names (as well as, of course, various special forms). The patterns are:

1   A limited number of nationalities in or near Europe. These have separate nouns for persons and for adjectives describing the nations and their nationals. These adjectives also usually serve secondary purposes as the names of national languages. In this group, the adjective ends in *-ish* or something similar.

Country	Adjective (and language where relevant)	Person
(Great) Britain	British	a Briton
England	English	an Englishman Englishwoman
Scotland	Scottish/Scots	a Scot Scotsman Scotswoman
Wales	Welsh	a Welshman Welshwoman
Ireland	Irish	an Irishman Irishwoman
France	French	a Frenchman Frenchwoman
Spain	Spanish	a Spaniard
Denmark	Danish	a Dane
Sweden	Swedish	a Swede
Poland	Polish	a Pole
Finland	Finnish	a Finn
Turkey	Turkish	a Turk

2 the vast majority of nations with Latin-type names, whose adjective and noun (and name of language, where relevant) are identical, ending in *-an* or *-ian*, presentable in the following groups:

Country	Adjective/person (and language, where relevant)
Cuba	Cuban
Jamaica	Jamaican
Kenya	Kenyan
Libya	Libyan
Venezuela	Venezuelan
Algeria	Algerian
Austria	Austrian
Colombia	Colombian
India	Indian
Russia	Russian
Syria	Syrian
Zambia	Zambian
Chile	Chilean
Hungary	Hungarian
Italy	Italian
Mexico	Mexican
Morocco	Moroccan
Paraguay	Paraguayan
Brazil	Brazilian
Ecuador	Ecuadorian
Egypt	Egyptian
Iran	Iranian
Jordan	Jordanian
Argentina	Argentinian
Belgium	Belgian
Canada	Canadian
Germany	German
Ghana	Ghanaian
Norway	Norwegian
Panama	Panamanian
Peru	Peruvian

3   A limited number of nationalities, mainly in eastern Asia, whose
adjective and noun (and name of language where relevant) are
identical, ending in -*ese*. Such national names generally have an
'n', 'm' or 'l' in them.

Country	Adjective/person (and language, where relevant)
Japan	Japanese
Nepal	Nepalese
Sudan	Sudanese
Vietnam	Vietnamese
Burma	Burmese
China	Chinese
Guyana	Guyanese
Malta	Maltese
Congo	Congolese
Lebanon	Lebanese
Portugal	Portuguese

(**Note** that some cities and regions also form their derivatives in
this way: *Vienna/Viennese*; *Genoa/Genoese*; *Faroes/Faroese*;
Canton/Cantonese, etc)

Some common exceptions to the above patterns are as follows:

Cyprus	Cypriot
Greece	Greek
Iceland	Icelander, *adj* Icelandic
Iraq	Iraqi
Israel	Israeli
Netherlands, the (Holland)	Dutchman/woman, *adj* Dutch
New Zealand	New Zealander, *attrib* New Zealand
Pakistan	Pakistani
Philippines, the	Filipino
Switzerland	Swiss
United States of America, the	American
Yugoslavia	Yugoslav, *sometimes* Yugoslavian

Using the preceding lists as both a source and a guide, complete the following exercises:

1   Below is a sentence frame with two blank spaces. Use the countries in the list that follows it to make ten complete sentences:

If a person comes from ＿＿＿＿＿, then he or she is ＿＿＿＿＿.

a.   China
b.   Uruguay
c.   Indonesia
d.   Iraq
e.   Greece

f.   Morocco
g.   Nigeria
h.   Peru
i.   Switzerland
j.   Turkey

2   Below is a second sentence frame with two blank spaces. Use the countries in the list that follows it to make ten complete sentences. You should note that plural forms (where they occur) are needed here. Additionally, adjective forms ending in *-ish* or something similar can often be used in such cases collectively to refer to a people (as, for example, *(the) British*).

If people come from ＿＿＿＿＿, then they are ＿＿＿＿＿.

a.   Scotland
b.   France
c.   England
d.   the U.S.A.
e.   Norway

f.   Iceland
g.   Ireland
h.   Cyprus
i.   Tanzania
j.   Japan

3   Write the name of a person from these countries:

a.   Wales   ＿＿＿＿
b.   Denmark   ＿＿＿＿
c.   Argentina ＿＿＿＿
d.   France   ＿＿＿＿
e.   Spain   ＿＿＿＿
f.   Belgium   ＿＿＿＿

4   Complete the following:

a.   The history of China is ＿＿＿＿＿ history.
b.   The language of Greece is the ＿＿＿＿＿ language.
c.   The art of Burma is ＿＿＿＿＿.
d.   The dialect spoken in Canton is known as the ＿＿＿＿＿.

e.   The customs of the people of Mexico are ＿＿＿＿＿.
f.   The history of Ireland is ＿＿＿＿＿.
g.   The empire created by the ancient Persians was called the ＿＿＿＿＿.

h.   A museum in the United States of America is an
     _____.

i.   Wine from Spain and Portugal is _____ and
     _____.

j.   Materials exported from East Germany, Poland and
     Hungary are _____.

5   Change each word in the first list below so that it can be used
    appropriately in the second list:

1	Malta	a.	_____ sausages
2	France	b.	_____ cigars
3	Egypt	c.	_____ perfume
4	Switzerland	d.	_____ sheep
5	Poland	e.	_____ crosses
6	Ireland	f.	_____ mythology
7	Cuba	g.	_____ pyramids
8	Brazil	h.	_____ whiskey
9	Greece	i.	_____ watches
10	Australia	j.	_____ coffee

Final note   Never forget that all forms of words connected with the
names of countries, cities, etc, begin in English with *capital letters*.

7.8 Editing a text: 'Swimming as a Sport'

The following passage discusses swimming as a sport, but is by no
means ready for publication. There are 10 faults of punctuation, 10
more spelling errors, and 10 grammatical slips. Edit the text.

As a sport, swimming can be very satisfying, you can, for
example, swim indoors or outdoor, as one of a team, or
alone. You can swim for physical fitness or for a challenge.
You can to swim to prove something or to win something or
to get somewhere or simply because you like the water.   5

For some people swiming is a pleasant but not very active
thing, to be enjoy on a sunny day at the beach with a picnic
afterwards. For others it is a highly competive business, even
a profession. It is a sport who demands hours of disciplined
practice.   10

Wether you become a once a-year holiday swimmer or a
famous international champion, you must had had a reason
to start in the first place. Perhaps your mother or father was

keen swimmers; perhaps you had an enthousiastic teacher at
school, perhaps your friends got you interesting. Like most   15
people, however you probably began at the shallow end of a
public swimming pool, and only after a lot of practice did
you get to the deep end, the diving board and finaly the
excitments of the open sea

Swimming of course is not only watersport today. There   20
are many: sailing, canoeing, waterskiing, surfing, dinghies
and the like. There is also a great varity of kinds of
swimming: shallow-water swimming, racing and diving in
the one hand, and deepsea swimming and diving with the aid
of flippers and aqualungs on the other hand. People who   25
enjoy these pastimes and professions do so because, like fish,
they feel at home in the water.

Feeling at home in the water means not only enjoyment of
water under good conditions, but also confidance and
courage under difficult conditions. There are dangers in the   30
water, whether or not it is the open sea. People can and do
drown even, capable swimmers who go beyond what they
can safely do. There are time when a good swimmer needs to
concentrate on saving his or her own life, or the life of
another person, who is in danger of drowning. Under such   35
conditions it is vital, not to panic and create uneccessary
problems for everybody. The rules for survival therefore
include keeping calm being able to float for a long time and
the hability to tread water while waiting to be rescued.

7.9 Controlled composition: 'Competitive Swimming'

Create a passage of one or two paragraphs from the basic material
printed below. It is a simple description of such things as swimming
competitions. If you wish, you may add additional material taken
from the previous passage (7.8), or from any other source. You may
add such material at the beginning, throughout the text, or at the
end, and should take particular care with your organization, layout
on the page, spelling, punctuation and grammar. If you do not
manage everything satisfactorily the first time, do the work again.

Most professional writers need to write their material more than once before they are satisfied with it.

1 interest/competitive/swimming/have/increase/enormous/all/level/recent/year

2 individual/have/compete/for/year/against/each/other/but/one/very/interest/new/thing/world/swimming/as/sport/be/growth/what/be/call/'age-group swimming'

3 this/kind/competition/begin/United States/1950s/and/have/now/spread/almost/every/country/world

4 in/each/country/there/be/national/govern/body/that/organize/various/form/competitive/swimming/other/watersport

5 competition/be/arrange/not/only/adult/but/also/young/swimmer/same/age/range

6 event/be/usual/arrange/two-year/step/example/12-year-old and 13-year-old/youngster/compete/group

7 racing distance/vary/according/age/group/and/some/place/such/Australia/even/very/young/competitor/be/give/chance/compete/over/fair/long/distance/up to/1,500/metre

8 most/swimming/club/now/have/age-group/team/and/arrange/special/training/practice/session/for/they

UNIT 8

8.1 Comprehension and composition model: 'The World of Skiing'

Photograph taken at the Col des Vaux below Mont Gelé, Switzerland.

Here is a passage describing in brief the history and present-day development of skiing. Read it twice, noting how the material is developed (every paragraph, in effect, dealing with a fresh aspect of the topic).

According to the *Advanced Learner's Dictionary of Current English* (Oxford University Press, 1974), a ski is 'one of a pair of

long, narrow strips of wood, strapped under the feet for moving
over snow'. The art of using such strips of wood is very old; indeed,
the earliest known 'picture' of a skier is a rock carving in Norway,   5
dating from 2,000 B.C. The oldest skis that have ever been found –
in bogs in Sweden and Finland – are thought to be between 4,000
and 5,000 years old. Skis may also have been used by the northern
Chinese about 300 B.C., and the Vikings of Scandinavia certainly
used them in the 10th and 11th centuries. They did not, however,   10
use them for sport. Northern Europeans used their skis for the
practical business of moving – and fighting – in winter lands.

Nowadays, there are basically two kinds of skiing:
1   *Nordic or cross-country skiing*, which may or may not be a
sport, and is essentially a way of getting about on snow, and   15
2   *Alpine or downhill skiing*, which developed in and around
Switzerland in the 19th century and is purely a sporting activity.

Nordic and Alpine have skis in common but little else (and even
the skis are not exactly the same). Nordic skiing is a way of
enjoying vast snowy panoramas; anyone who enjoys walking in   20
mountain areas will also probably enjoy this means of locomotion.
It is excellent for touring: uphill, downhill, over flat land, over
frozen lakes and along forest trails. Alpine skiing, on the other
hand, is big wintertime vacation business with a technology of its
own: ski-resorts, ski-lifts and even snow-flattening machines. It has   25
its own special vocabulary, skills and competitions, and is a
significant holiday industry in such countries as Switzerland,
Austria, Canada, the United States, Italy and Scotland. It can
provide the feeling of flying like a snowbird – or of breaking a leg.

Whatever kind one prefers, skiing is a sport for anyone who is   30
normally active. There are no barriers of age or sex: women do as
well as men and often a slim girl proves more competent than a
muscular man in his prime. A middle-aged mother may make
neater turns than a nervous youngster, and children (if they start
young) can race down mountainsides at high speeds in no greater   35
danger than on their bicycles in city streets. To be expert, however,
means practice and knowledge; good skiers have learned to read
the snow, and to change their style as they move from one quality
of snow to another.

Skiing can cost a lot of money. Costs can, however, be cut by   40
hiring not only the skis and poles but also the boots, anoraks and
ski-clothes. The cost of hiring such articles varies from 10 to 50
percent of the purchase price over a fortnight's holiday. It is a
particularly good idea to hire children's clothing. This should be
done, preferably, at the ski-resort, where one gets the added   45
advantage that hired equipment can be changed if it does not work
or fit properly.

But why ski? Some people love the lightness and the thrill of

speed, of flying on their slim skis through sunlit mountain passes
and down long dizzy slopes. Others enjoy the social life before,   50
during and especially after the skiing itself. Others still, however,
just need their skis for getting around in remote areas; for them it is,
and always has been, an everyday wintertime necessity.

Below are some statements relating to the passage. Some are true (T)
in terms of the passage, while others are false (F). Mark them
appropriately, and if a statement is false, say why.

a. ☐ The art of skiing is thought to be about 6,000 years old.

b. ☐ People in ancient China probably used skis.

c. ☐ Alpine skiing needs different equipment from Nordic skiing.

d. ☐ If you take part in Nordic skiing you do not go down hillsides.

e. ☐ Nordic skiing is excellent for touring.

f. ☐ Alpine skiing is an important holiday industry in at least four
European countries.

g. ☐ Anyone who is normally active can learn to ski.

h. ☐ Men tend to be better at skiing than women.

i. ☐ You can avoid much of the expense of skiing by hiring your
equipment at a ski-resort.

j. ☐ There are essentially two kinds of skiers: those who enjoy the
skiing itself, and those who enjoy the company of other skiers.

8.2 Spelling:
Completing words

Below are ten extracts taken directly from the passage. In each
sentence there is one or more word with some letters missing. The
missing parts of the words are indicated by a dash (_____). No
indication is given of the number of possible missing letters.
Complete each word properly spelled.

a. A_____ding to the 'Advanced Learner's Dict_____y of Current
English' (Oxford University Press, 1974), a ski is 'one of a pair of
long, narrow strips of wood, str_____d under the feet for moving
over snow'.

b. North_____ Eur_____s used th_____ skis for the practical b_____ss
of moving, and fighting, in winter lands.

c. Alpine or downhill sk_____, which dev_____ed in and around
Switzerland in the 19th century and is purely a sporting activity.

d. It is ex____t for touring.

e. Whatever kind one pr____rs, sk____ is a sport for anyone who is norm____ active.

f. There are no bar____s of age or sex: women do as well as men and often a slim girl proves more compet____ than a mus____r man in his prime.

g. . . . and children (if they start young) can race down m____nsides at high speeds in no greater danger than on their b____cles in city streets.

h. To be expert, however, means pract____ and kn____l____e.

i. The cost of hiring such articles v____s from 10 to 50 p____cent of the p____chase price over a fortnight's holiday.

j. This should be done, pr____ably, at the ski-resort, where one gets the added a____tage that hired equip____ can be changed if it does not work or fit prop____.

8.3 Vocabulary definition:
Consulting dictionaries

There are many dictionaries of English available today. These include:

1 bilingual dictionaries (French–English, Spanish–English, Japanese–English, etc, published by many companies)

2 dictionaries for native users of the language, published by, for example, Oxford, Chambers, Merriam-Webster and Random House

3 dictionaries specially prepared (and completely in English) for foreign learners and users of the language, published by Oxford, Longman, Chambers and Collins.

It is often interesting and useful to compare the ways in which different dictionaries describe the same word. It is also useful to see how differently dictionaries organize their presentation of information about words. To get the most out of a dictionary, one needs to know something about its organization, and one way to do this is to compare several dictionaries (also looking carefully at their introductory descriptions of themselves).

Below is a list of ten words used in the passage about skiing. They are fairly typical words of the English language. Try to find one copy (at least) of each kind of dictionary mentioned above and look up the words below, making notes about what you find:

a. barrier   (line 31)   f.   purchase   (l. 43)
b. hire   (l. 44)   g.   slim   (l. 32)
c. locomotion   (l. 21)   h.   strip   (l. 3)
d. muscular   (l. 33)   i.   technology   (l. 24)
e. practice   (l. 37)   j.   trail   (l. 23)

8.4   Grammar and vocabulary: Compound words

Look at the following paragraph taken from the passage on skiing where the abbreviations n = noun and v = verb.

> Nordic and Alpine have skis in common but little else (and even the skis are not exactly the same). Nordic skiing is a way of enjoying vast snowy panoramas; anyone who enjoys walking in *mountain areas* (n + n) will also probably enjoy this means of locomotion. It is excellent for touring: uphill, downhill, over flat land, over frozen lakes and along *forest trails* (n + n). Alpine skiing, on the other hand, is big *wintertime vacation business* ((n + n) + n + n) with a technology of its own: *ski-resorts* (n + n), *ski-lifts* (n + n) and even *snow-flattening machines* ((n + v) + n). It has its own special vocabulary, skills and competitions, and is a significant *holiday industry* (n + n) in such countries as *Switzerland* (also, in fact, n + n), Austria, Canada, the *United States* (v + n), Italy and *Scotland* (n + n). It can provide the feeling of flying like a *snowbird* (n + n) – or of breaking a leg.

The groups of words *italicized* in the extract can all be described as 'compound words'. The commonest compound words are noun/noun combinations (like *mountain areas* and *wintertime vacation business*), but quite often verbs and adjectives are also involved (as, for example, in *United States* and *blackboard*). In such combinations, the first word element serves to give precise information about the second word element, and so on. Thus:

1   What kind of *area* is it? – It is a *mountain area*.
2   What kind of *trails* are they? – They are *forest trails*.
3   What kind of *business* is it? – It is *vacation business*.

4   What kind of *time* is it? – It is *wintertime*.

5   What kind of *vacation business* is it? – It is *wintertime vacation business*.

6   What kind of *resorts* and *lifts* are they? – They are *ski-resorts* and *ski-lifts*.

7   What kind of *machines* are they? – They are *snow-flattening machines* (that is, machines that flatten snow).

8   What *lands* are they – They are *Switzerland* (the land of the Swiss, slightly altered), and *Scotland* (the land of the Scots).

9   What kind of *states* are they? – They are the *United States* (of America).

10   What kind of *bird* is it? – It is a *snowbird*.

Note that when saying such compounds aloud in answer to the questions, native users of English will stress the first word-element. This is typical of the way most compounds are generally pronounced. Practice doing it. In writing, compounds may be written as one word (like *snowbird*), as two or more words with hyphens (like *ski-resort*) or with the elements side by side (like *mountain areas*). There are no clear rules in English in this matter, but there are certain tendencies: Shorter words tend to be put together, words that would look odd together may be hyphenated (like *ski-lift* rather than *skilift*), but the great majority of compounds today consist on paper of separate words. Wide reading is probably the best and simplest way to becoming accustomed to current usage.

Below are two sentence frames: a question and an answer. Provide ten questions and ten suitable answers by using the two lists below, matching the words in the first column with those in the second column.

What kind of _____ is it? It is a _____ _____.

1	pot	a.	swimming
2	house	b.	football
3	factory	c.	business
4	brush	d.	sheepskin
5	address	e.	steam **or** steam-driven
6	bridge	f.	country
7	coat	g.	soap-making
8	engine	h.	steel
9	pool	i.	flower
10	match	j.	tooth

8.5 Grammar and vocabulary: The art of using numbers

Numbers are used for many different purposes: general arithmetic, buying and selling, listing things, giving sizes and quantities, for addresses, dates and ages, and so on. The following exercises are intended to provide practice in using increasingly complex expressions containing numbers.

Number work:
First stage

Study and say aloud the following groups of numbers:

1 4   14   40   144   1,440   1440 A.D.

2 9   19   90   990   1,984   1984 A.D.   a 1984 car

3 4th   9th   ¼   ⅑   0.4   9.04

4 24th   29th   345th   1st   31st   441st

5 14 houses   the 14th house   a 14-year-old house
   a 14th-century house   a 400-year-old book

6 45%   99%   99.9%   2%   2.5%

7 £234   £23,345   £456,364   £3,987,004

8 $984 $7,654 $298,456 $8,926,386

9 031 227 8686 (a British telephone number)
   01   667 2245

10 In 1974 Oxford University Press published a dictionary for foreign learners of English, containing over 100,000 items in phonetic transcription, 50,000 main words and derivatives, 11,000 idiomatic expressions and 1,000 illustrations. The original version of this dictionary came out in 1948, a second edition in 1963, so that the 1974 edition is, in fact, the third. A special revised version of this third edition was published in 1980.

Number work:
Second stage

Many compound expressions in English contain numbers. Study the examples below, then complete the sentences that follow in appropriate ways.

Example 1   The wall is thirty feet high.
   ▷   It is therefore a thirty-foot wall.
                30-foot wall.

Example 2   The man is thirty years old.
   ▷   He is therefore a thirty-year-old man.
                30-year-old man.

Example 3   The car was made in the year 1982.
   ▷   It is therefore a 1982 car/model.

Example 4   The house was built in the nineteenth century.
   ▷   It is therefore a nineteenth-century house.
                19th-century house.

Note

1   Nouns that are plural in their normal grammatical positions become *singular* when used as the first elements in compounds. This is an almost universal rule for compound words.

2   One could say 'a 30-foot-high wall' and might sometimes need to, but when people discuss walls they are generally concerned with height, and so the adjective is not necessary. With the ages of people and things, however, it is normal practice to keep the adjective 'old' in the compound form.

a.   The wall is fifteen feet high. It is therefore a . . .
b.   The boat is forty feet long. It is therefore a . . .
c.   The truck weighs ten tons. It is a . . .
d.   The tanker weighs 12,000 tons, so it is a . . .
e.   The plan covers 45 years, so it is a . . .
f.   The project will continue for ten years. It is a . . .
g.   The boy is thirteen years old. He is a . . .
h.   The bank manager is 35 years old. He is therefore a . . .
i.   The baby is eight weeks old. He/She/It is an . . .
j.   The dispute between them is now 17 years old. It is a . . .
k.   The fossil is 70 million years old, so it is a . . .
l.   The engine was built in 1949. It is therefore a . . .

113

m.   That particular model was produced in 1977. It is a . . .

n.   There were two designs: the 1980 design and the one produced in 1982. We much prefer the . . .

o.   That edition of the dictionary came out in 1974, so it is known as the . . .

p.   The club was founded in 1972, so people call it the . . .

q.   That house was built in the 15th century; it is a . . .

r.   The manuscript dates from the seventh century, so it is a . . .

s.   The castle was built in the 14th century. It is a . . .

t.   The students are now in their fourth year at college. They are . . .

u.   The factory manager is 50 years old and lives in a house built in the 18th century, so . . .

v.   The boat is 50 feet long and was built in 1980, so it is a . . .

8.6 Punctuation:
Numbers in a text

Punctuate the following passage. It describes the history of one of the world's most famous dictionaries.

when the oxford english dictionary also known as the new english dictionary and murrays dictionary was first published in 1928 it was already 71 years old its story actually began in the year 1857 when a learned clergyman richard chenevix trench spoke to the philological society in england about various deficiencies in the dictionaries of the time the society decided not long afterwards to create an entirely new kind of dictionary that would provide the life histories of as many english words as possible but its members hardly appreciated that the task would take so long and that by 1928 their employees would have collected and defined no less than 414825 words the dictionary had a succession of eminent editors four englishmen herbert coleridge frederick furnival henry bradley and c t onions and two scotsmen james murray and william craigie volunteers from all over the world helped in the enterprise and worked unbelievably hard on it a mr austin is said to have sent in 165000 quotations a mr douglas 136000 and a dr helwich of vienna some 50000 in 1879 when murray succeeded furnival in leading the project he took over from him 1¾ tons of material and that was only halfway between the birth and the completion of the work

8.7 Punctuation:
Variety in a text

A well-written text or passage will contain a wide variety of devices connected with grammar, usage, style and logic. Punctuation is, of course, particularly important in the business of making a passage clear and easy to read. The passage on skiing contains quite a variety of material, and therefore has a relatively complex pattern of punctuation. In order to establish this point clearly, go back to the passage and find the following:

1 one reference to a published book (noting how the reference is presented)

2 one quotation from a book (noting how the quotation is fitted into the flow of the passage)

3 one use of quotation marks to present an ordinary everyday word in a special way

4 two uses of the semi-colon (bringing two distinct sentences into a particularly close relationship)

5 two uses of commas for parenthesis

6 two uses of brackets for parenthesis

7 two uses of dashes for parenthesis

8 one example of a dash used for dramatic effect

9 two lists of three or more items each

10 one example of a question that the writer answers (on the assumption that a reader might have been asking it)

8.8 Grammar:
Personal pronouns used impersonally

Personal pronouns (such as *I, you, he, she, they,* etc) usually refer directly to the person concerned. Compare, however, the following:

1 I prefer Nordic skiing and he prefers Alpine.

2 'Do whatever you prefer,' she said.

3 Whatever kind you prefer, skiing is a sport for anyone who is normally active.

4 Whatever kind one prefers, skiing is a sport for anyone who is normally active.

In the first and second examples, the pronouns (*I, he, you, she*) pose no problems. In the third example, however, the pronoun *you* could mean either a particular person or group of persons, *or* people generally. Without further context the meaning of the pronoun is not clear. (This in fact is often the case in English, forcing people to ask: 'Excuse me, do you mean me or anybody?') In the fourth example, the pronoun *one* strongly suggests 'anybody' (although some people do use this pronoun in order to talk about themselves without using *I* and *me*). Where *you* and *one* are clearly used to talk about people generally, *you* tends to be less formal and *one* to be more formal and impersonal:

5   If you do these things well, you can really enjoy yourself.   **less formal**

6   If one does these things well, one can really enjoy oneself.   **more formal and impersonal**

There is a slight difference in practice as regards the pronoun *one* in Britain and in North America. In Britain, *one* is repeated throughout the statement, but in North America generally the statement begins with *one* but then goes on with *he/him*:

7   Whatever one prefers, one should always take care.   **British**

8   Whatever one prefers, he should always take care.   **North American**

Using these notes and examples as a guide, make each of the following sentences more or less formal as necessary:

a.   You can always hire skiing equipment at the resort if you want to. You can save quite a lot of money that way.
(**Note**   If you wish to re-express this section in the North American style, it is better to change the word 'hire' to 'rent'. In British English one 'hires' people and smaller, more mobile things and 'rents' accommodation or land; in North American English one 'hires' people and 'rents' everything else.)

b.   One should always try to read the quality of the snow and change one's style accordingly.

c.   1   British style
     2   North American style
You might suppose that skiing is quite a modern activity, with a relatively short history. If you supposed that, you would be wrong.

d.   'One meets all one's friends at the ski-resort,' she said.

e.   Some people prefer cross-country skiing; others prefer downhill skiing. Whatever one's preference, both are excellent forms of exercise.

f.   'Well, if one must go, one must go,' said the king, unhappily.

8.9 Vocabulary: The right word in the right place

In the passage below there are fifteen blank spaces, numbered appropriately. Following the passage are fifteen sets of three words or phrases each, also numbered. Choose the word from each set that best fits the passage.

The modern ski is (1)_____ wonderful tool. It is specially built (2)_____ you (3)_____ easily turn and control (4)_____ speed as you go downhill. Beginners are always surprised (5)_____ they find out how quickly speed builds (6)_____ on skis. In five or six seconds a beginner can feel quite (7)_____ control. Driving a car (8)_____ 60 m.p.h. does not feel as fast or as dangerous (9)_____ 10 m.p.h. (10)_____ skis. And it is this quick build-up (11)_____ speed (12)_____ makes the art of turning (13)_____ important. Turning the skis controls the speed and (14)_____ the only way to slow (15)_____ or stop.

(1)   one, the, a
(2)   so that, in order, so as
(3)   could, can, will
(4)   your, the, its
(5)   when, while, as
(6)   out, up, over
(7)   away from, beyond, out of
(8)   on, at, with
(9)   than, as, to
(10) in, with, on
(11) to, of, for
(12) where, who, that
(13) such, so, as
(14) will be, is, would be
(15) down, in, back

8.10 Controlled composition: A sport, hobby or pastime

Like all the texts used as models in this course, the passage on skiing has a distinctive shape. It is developed in a particular way that makes use of its content and its language resources to achieve a particular effect. It is intended to create an interest in skiing in the reader. The vocabulary, grammar, punctuation and stylistic devices all work together to achieve this effect; you, the reader, can judge best whether in fact it does achieve that effect. It is, however, only one of many possible ways of describing a topic, all equally good in the hands of a careful writer. Below you will find the outline of the basic structure of the passage. It is not, however, restricted to skiing – or to football. This structure can be used for any sport, hobby, pastime or similar topic. Choose one, and use the structure shown here as a 'skeleton' on which to build your own description.

Possible language items	Suggestions about the topic
1 'According to . . .'	Your introduction, using a source book and a quotation to define your subject (or some part of it)
2 'X is (not) very old . . .'	Some historical details
3 'There are basically n kinds of X (today) . . .'	Any classification of the topic that seems reasonable; special subdivisions (if any)
4 'X_1 and X_2 (etc) are . . .'	Further descriptive details; any useful geographical points (if any)
5 'Whatever kind one prefers (etc) . . .'	Further details related to human interest (that is, where actual people come in)
6 'X costs/does not cost (etc) a lot of money . . .'	Practical comments and suggestions (if any)
7 'But why . . .?'	Conclusion, giving reasons, comments etc relating to doing (or not doing) whatever it is

UNIT 9   Revision

9.1   Comprehension and composition model: 'The Cinematic Art'

Photograph 'Hot Shot East-bound at Iaegar, West Virginia, USA', taken by
O. Winston Link in 1956, in the permanent collection of the Museum of
Modern Art, New York City.

Here is a passage describing the film industry. Read it twice, noting
how the material is developed and considering the grammar,
vocabulary, punctuation and layout.

For the first half of the 20th century the cinema dominated all other
forms of popular entertainment in the world. During the heyday of
the 'movie theatre' or the 'picture house' – as the Americans and
British variously called their cinema halls – millions of people
throughout the world developed the habit (almost the addiction) of

5

going to see a film at least once a week. This was the golden age of
Hollywood, film capital of both the United States and the world.

The first silent films (in black and white, of course) were shown
during the 1890s as part of music-hall entertainment, taking turns
along with various live acts such as singers, dancers and magicians.   10
Such films were simply to give the audience a thrill; the vision of a
huge locomotive racing towards you out of the screen usually
produced the effect that both the promoter and the audience
desired. Indeed, this thrill element continues to be very significant in
movies, as is witnessed by the demand for more and more   15
spectacular 'special effects' in various science-fiction extravaganzas.

A Frenchman, Georges Méliès, created the first actual story-
related movies around 1900 and the first American story film was
The Great Train Robbery in 1903. From then until 1914, American
and European film-makers were more or less equal, but after the   20
outbreak of the First World War Europeans had other more
pressing concerns, and far away in California, near the city of Los
Angeles, the film-makers of the New World went ahead on their
own, producing first the 'talkies' and then 'technicolor'. Many
European countries (including France, Britain, Russia and   25
Germany) have continued to make films, but they have never really
managed to catch up with the lead that Hollywood established
during and after the Great War.

The only nation that can nowadays be said to rival the United
States in the volume of films produced, money made and numbers   30
entertained is India, which has an extremely successful home and
export business in films; it makes movies available both to Indian
communities established in other parts of the world and to
countries whose people are culturally closer to Bombay than to
Hollywood.   35

The cinema, since its inception, has been in direct competition
with a variety of other forms of entertainment. These include:
participating in and watching sports and games, acting in or going
to the live theatre, performing for or listening to radio, watching
television, and – most recently – playing video games. The live   40
theatre has not done particularly well in the face of competition
from the cinema, while in turn the cinema has not done too well
when faced with the domestic miracle of millions of private screens
in people's own homes. Looking back at the way in which
television has displaced the movies since the early 1950s, we might   45
even say that the cinema was the dinosaur ancestor of TV, rather
than that TV is a miniature cinema.

The only clear advantage that the public movie has over the
private tube is the size of the picture offered. Even that advantage

may not last much longer, however, as more and more people in   50
affluent parts of the world become interested in large TV wall
screens for their living rooms.

   Not, of course, that Hollywood is going to stop making films; the
TV companies will need them for a long time to come, as will the
videotape industry. The framing of celluloid dreams goes on, with   55
whole galaxies of 'stars', 'starlets' and 'superstars' whom we can
watch, love, hate, envy or disdain (according to our inclinations). It
is a state of affairs that could never have been imagined in, say,
1839, the year when Sir John Herschel first offered the world the
term 'photography'.   60

1   Are the following statements true (T) or false (F), in terms of the
    passage? If a statement is false, say why.

    a. ☐ The cinema was the primary medium of entertainment in
          the world during the first fifty years of this century.

    b. ☐ Americans used to call a hall for showing films a 'picture
          house'.

    c. ☐ The element that was most important in films in the 1890s
          is no longer very significant in film-making.

    d. ☐ The outbreak of the 1914–18 war had a major impact on
          the international film industry.

    e. ☐ No nation today comes anywhere near the United States in
          the production and commercial distribution of films.

    f. ☐ The cinema competes directly with the live theatre and
          usually wins in terms of numbers taking an interest in these
          forms of entertainment.

    g. ☐ Television and the cinema also compete directly, and here
          again the cinema has managed to hold its own.

    h. ☐ Although the large screen is a feature that still attracts
          people to the cinema certain technical advances in TV
          presentation may change this and draw people away from
          the cinema.

    i. ☐ Hollywood has failed to change its style so as to take
          advantage of the market presented by domestic television.

    j. ☐ People regularly become emotionally involved in various
          ways with the stars and stories that they follow on their
          screens, or at least so the passage suggests.

2   Try to find the following:

   a.   all the examples of parenthesis using dashes that occur in the passage

   b.   all the examples of parenthesis using brackets that occur in the passage

   c.   all examples of parenthesis using commas that occur in the passage

   d.   all examples of special words presented to the reader in quotation marks

   e.   all examples of the use of semi-colons

   f.   all examples of a definite article being used with a singular noun to indicate a type (like *the cat* or *the rose*)

   g.   all subordinate clauses beginning with a relative pronoun

   h.   two compound sentences expressing a comparison by using *but*, both in the same paragraph

   i.   any ten compound words used in the passage

   j.   the point at which the passage turns from straight historical description to more contemporary matters

9.2   Vocabulary definition:
Consulting dictionaries

Using a dictionary (preferably unilingual English, preferably intended for learners of the language), look up the following words. Check the meanings against the ways in which the words have been used in the text, and then put each word in a sentence of your own.

a.   heyday   (line 2)
b.   addiction   (line 5)
c.   thrill   (lines 11 and 14)
d.   locomotive   (line 12)
e.   promoter   (line 13)
f.   spectacular   (line 16)
g.   extravaganza   (line 16)
h.   pressing   (line 22)
i.   volume   (line 30)
j.   inception   (line 36)
k.   video   (line 40)
l.   miracle   (line 43)
m.   dinosaur   (line 46)
n.   miniature   (line 47)
o.   affluent   (line 51)

9.3 Grammar and organization: Logical order

There is almost always a simple logical order in the sentences of a passage. Below you will find two similar exercises. Each has a set of sentences which make up a continuous text. The sentences, however, are not in their proper order. Re-arrange them so that the passages can be read properly.

1 'CinemaScope'

A. Chrétien used a special photographic lens to 'squeeze' a wide picture on to standard 35-millimetre film then, by using a special projection lens, restored the image on the wide screen without distortion.

B. The film companies had therefore succeeded all too well in their original aim.

C. This wide-screen technique was invented by the French physicist Henri Chrétien in the late 1920s.

D. The very thing that made CinemaScope films attractive in the first place, however, now began to make them unattractive, because these wide-screen films could not be satisfactorily adapted for TV display.

E. CinemaScope is the trade name for a technique that projects a motion picture on to a screen that is two and a half times wider than it is high.

F. This remarkable invention was ignored, however, until the major film studios began to feel threatened by the growing success of television.

G. This innovation proved effective for some years, but later posed problems because television companies are willing to pay in order to re-use cinema films on TV, and film companies are willing to do business with them.

H. They then developed the technique as a means of attracting people back to the cinema by offering them a spectacular new visual experience impossible to reproduce on a domestic TV screen.

2 'A Road Accident'

A. It involved a car and a truck at an intersection with traffic lights.

B. Meanwhile, a little red sports car came racing along the other way.

C. Road accidents can happen all too easily.

D. Amazingly enough, nobody was killed, but the passenger in the sports car was badly injured and several people in the shop suffered badly from shock.

E. There was a particularly bad accident in our town not so long ago, the kind of accident that need never happen.

F. He must have been in a hurry.

G. The lights had changed to red and, quite reasonably, the stationary truck began to move.

H. The truck hit the car and sent it spinning into the window of a corner shop with three or four people in it.

I. The driver tried to jump the lights and beat the truck.

9.4 Punctuation, grammar and organization: Logic and layout

This section is similar to the previous one. It is also in two parts. The first part contains material that is also wrongly ordered, but in addition this material is not yet punctuated. You must first punctuate it fully, then re-arrange it to make sense. The second part takes us back to the explorers on the river Zaire in Africa, and requires to be fully punctuated and attractively laid out.

1 'Why Do Birds Sing?'

A. he turned to his mother who was sitting on a chair beside him and asked why does that little bird sing

B. high in the trees at the bottom of the garden a bird was singing magnificently

C. you do ask such odd questions his mother said with a sigh

D. why does it sing she slowly repeated very puzzled well I suppose its because its happy dear

E. a boy of about seven was lying on the grass fascinated by the bird

F. but surely it doesnt just sing when its happy what does it do when its sad or angry or lonely

G. he realized suddenly that parents dont have all the answers to lifes questions it took years for him to find out why birds sing because most people just have no idea why

2 'Journey down the Zaire'

colonel snells expedition did not find the journey down the zaire very easy they were chased by elephants surrounded by snakes fell sick with fever and were often in real danger on the river itself from currents that went in many directions from foaming rapids and from great whirlpools snell said about the journey it was rather like going by small boat from london to teheran he said that they never knew for sure what was round the next bend in the river because their maps were not particularly accurate he compared the zaire itelf to a powerful animal the worst moment he said was when a huge wave suddenly arose we went straight into it I thought we were going down there was an unbelievable whirlpool big enough to swallow a bus we only just escaped it our engine nearly stopped working we made it by about two seconds and I saw huge trees going down into the hole of the whirlpool it was like water running out of the bath the expedition was made up of both men and women one of the women a nurse said at times it was frightening on the rapids but it was exciting to know you were the first people to go over them she was asked by a journalist how the men had felt about having women with them on the trip I think they were a bit annoyed at first she answered but later they accepted us that was probably all to the good because the journey took four months and covered 2700 miles

9.5 Vocabulary: The right word in the right place

Below is a passage describing the story of Aladdin, in *The Thousand and One Nights*. There are, however, twenty blanks in the passage, each numbered. At the end of the passage, you will find twenty sets of words. In each set, there are three words that could fit in an appropriate blank, and each of these words has a letter (a,b,c). You must decide which word is the most suitable for its blank, which could serve as a second choice, and which is the least suitable. The first set is done for you, as an example.

The story of Aladdin and his wonderful lamp is a richly (1)_____ fantasy, ranging over both real and imaginary landscapes and with

characters that are much larger than life. Geographically, its
(2)_____ reaches from China to Africa, while imaginatively it
can tolerate strangely lit underground treasure-houses as well as the
(3)_____ of a (4)_____ palace from one continent to another
in the (5)_____ of an eye. Additionally, Aladdin is himself
socially interesting, because he is the poor boy who (6)_____,
with a little natural (7)_____ and a lot of magical assistance, to
become one of the richest men in the world and the husband of the
most (8)_____ princess in China.

There is nothing particularly kind and gentle about the story and
its characters. Take, for example, the (9)_____ when Aladdin,
with the help of a magic ring, (10)_____ his stolen wife and
palace to Africa, where the Magician, his enemy, has brought them
through the (11)_____ of the stolen lamp.

Aladdin meets the Princess secretly and gives her a little bag. He
tells her:

'Tomorrow, (12)_____ the Magician to supper. At the first
(13)_____, empty this bag into his cup, but don't put any of it
anywhere near your own food or drink.'

The Princess does as she is told, (14)_____ a most attractive
meal for the (15)_____ Magician, who quite happily and
unsuspectingly drinks the poison and drops dead. Aladdin is then
able to (16)_____ his lost lamp and (17)_____ his princess,
his palace, the lamp and himself to their (18)_____ home in the
East.

The story has all the colour, (19)_____ and unreality of a
dream. Like a dream, it allows people to get away, (20)_____,
from their everyday lives, which are not so colourful and dramatic. It
is, in other words, escapism in its purest form.

			b	c	a
(1)	a. built b. woven c. constructed				
(2)	a. act b. action c. activity		—	—	—
(3)	a. moving b. transfer c. transportation		—	—	—
(4)	a. whole b. complete c. full		—	—	—
(5)	a. blinking b. flash c. twinkling		—	—	—
(6)	a. succeeds b. manages c. proceeds		—	—	—
(7)	a. cleverness b. cunning c. art		—	—	—
(8)	a. beautiful b. pretty c. charming		—	—	—
(9)	a. point b. instant c. occasion		—	—	—
(10)	a. chases b. follows c. traces		—	—	—
(11)	a. power b. ability c. magic		—	—	—
(12)	a. bring b. call c. invite		—	—	—
(13)	a. moment b. opportunity c. chance		—	—	—
(14)	a. cooking b. making c. preparing		—	—	—

(15)   a. bad   b. wicked   c. ugly   — — —
(16)   a. regain   b. re-possess   c. restore   — — —
(17)   a. restore   b. return   c. replace   — — —
(18)   a. rightful   b. private   c. proper   — — —
(19)   a. drama   b. magic   c. strength   — — —
(20)   a. a little   b. briefly   c. shortly   — — —

9.6 Vocabulary: Forming words

Study the examples, then complete the sentences in the same way. You will need to form an adjective, an adverb or a noun. You will also sometimes need to use a prefix in addition to, or instead of, using one or more suffixes.

Example 1   She painted the picture in _____ colours.   **nature**
   ▷   She painted the picture in natural colours.

Example 2   Usually he talks a lot, but tonight he was _____ silent.   **nature**
   ▷   Usually he talks a lot, but tonight he was unnaturally silent.

a.   She is young, but she has a very _____ approach towards younger children.   **mother**

b.   What a _____ place this is!   **noise**

c.   He thought that I didn't like him, so he was _____ to me in return.   **friend**

d.   The doctor said that the patient was not only _____ but also dangerous.   **sane**

e.   They did not offer him the job because they thought that he was _____ of doing good work.   **capable**

f.   He drove the car _____ and caused a serious accident.   **care**

g.   She used to be a member of the team, but now she works _____.   **depend**

h.   The police accused him of being a _____ of stolen goods.   **reccive**

i.   The dancer moved across the stage in a _____, _____ way.   **noise**
    cat

127

j.   The pilot of the plane flew it _____.   **skill**

k.   She accused him of having a _____,   **stone**
     _____ heart.   **romance**

l.   He went _____ because of the hot,   **shirt**
     _____ weather.   **sun**

m.   Very little _____, _____ work could be   **use**
     done because of the bad weather.   **science**

n.   The animal was large and looked _____, but   **anger**
     in fact it was _____ _____ and had never   **perfect**
     been known to hurt anybody.   **harm**

o.   He spoke sadly about the _____ of getting   **possible**
     the work done in time, because, no matter how   **care**
     _____ they worked, they had _____   **sufficient**
     money and resources.

p.   To the _____ eye, the diamond looked   **train**
     _____, but the expert said that, if examined   **flaw**
     _____, anyone would be able to see a   **microscope**
     number of _____ _____.   **fortune**
                                                                                                  perfect

q.   The lawyer said that it was not only _____   **profession**
     and _____ to do what they suggested – it   **practice**
     was also _____ and _____ _____ to   **intelligent**
     succeed. He therefore refused.   **total**
                                                                                                  likely

r.   His father was a _____ _____ figure at   **power**
     the _____ level, but he was not at all   **politics**
     interested in matters of that kind, his whole time   **nation**
     being taken up with _____ and _____   **mathematics**
     research.   **technique**

s.   _____, he felt full of _____ when he   **norm**
     took part in _____ competitions, but on that   **confident**
     occasion he felt _____ _____ of himself,   **athlete**
     could not seem to do anything properly, and   **credible**
     consequently failed to do _____ to himself.   **sure**
                                                                                                  just

t.   She tried to look at the matter _____, to see   **emotion**
     it as a _____ problem that belonged to   **psychology**
     someone else, although in _____ terms it   **practice**
     proved _____ difficult to examine herself   **exception**
     _____.   **person**

128

9.7 Composition:
Your own topic(s)

For a time, following someone else's guidance in writing is useful, but no one would like to do it forever. It is important, however, to emphasize the need for shape and logic in writing any kind of story, report or description (even one which *seems* to have no shape or logic, like Lewis Carroll's *Alice in Wonderland*).

At this stage in the course you can now proceed to write more freely. If you wish to do so, you can follow the models presented here closely, or you can be more independent. You will still probably need plenty of practice. Depending upon the time available to you, write one, two, five or even ten compositions around the following themes, *or* on any subject that interests you, *or* any subject that you agree upon with your tutor. The themes of this course are:

1   an animal, animals, plants, objects
2   a journey, travel in general, people and places
3   war and peace, danger, adventure
4   myths and legends, stories using animals to say something about human beings
5   an accident, sudden strange events, witnessing something happen, reporting something that has happened
6   life, love, marriage, special customs around the world
7   a sport, hobby or pastime; special activities
8   a technical description of a thing, activity
9   a historical and social review of something like the cinema, television, fashion, art, literature

Answers

UNIT 1

1.1
a. **F:** Cats are not so completely domestic as dogs.
b. **F:** *Cats* like to keep some secrets.
c. **T**
d. **F:** The ancient Egyptians regarded cats as goddesses.
e. **T**
f. **T**
g. **F:** A woman is called a 'cat' if she speaks unkindly about other *women*.
h. **T**

1.2
a. no doubling: *kinder*
b. doubling: *swimmer, swimming*
c. no doubling: *coming*
d. no doubling: *reckoning*
e. doubling: *planned, planning*
f. doubling: *fatter, fattest*
g. no doubling: *naming*
h. no doubling: *developed, developing, development*
i. no doubling: *quieter*
j. doubling: *occurred, occurrence, occurring*
k. *British* doubling: *levelled, levelling*
   American no doubling: *leveled, leveling*
l. no doubling: *determination, determined*
m. doubling: *nodded, nodding*
n. doubling for *-ed* and *-ing*: *preferred, preferring*
   no doubling for: *preference, preferential, preferable*
o. *British* doubling: *gossipped, gossipping*
   American no doubling: *gossiped, gossiping*
p. doubling: *permitted, permitting*

If you have any doubts about how to spell words like these, study the following rules:

1 Normally the spelling of a base word is not changed when a suffix is added to it:

Bases ending in:

two vowels and a consonant
keep : keeper
lion : lioness

two consonants
host : hostess
own : owner

consonant(s) + e
wise : wisest
strange : stranger

2 Similarly, when a suffix begins with a written consonant no changes occur:

man : manly   woman : womanhood

3 There are, however, some changes to be made when a suffix begins with a written vowel and is added to a base that ends in a vowel and a consonant. In such cases, the final consonant is usually doubled:

big : bigger   hot : hottest
god : goddess   pet : petted

4 If a base word ends in certain less common consonants (such as *c, h, j, q, w* and *x*) doubling does not usually take place.

5 If a base word has two or more *spoken* syllables and the last syllable is *not* stressed, then the final consonant is *not* doubled:

*wan*der : wanderer   *rea*son : reasoning
*mur*der : murderer   *special* : specialist

6 This rule works well for American spelling

generally and most of the time for British spelling, but in British English such words ending in *l* and *p* get double consonants:

travel : traveler (*American*); traveller (*British*)

worship : worshiper (*American*): worshipper (*British*)

7 In base words with two or more spoken syllables where the last syllable *is* stressed, doubling takes place in both American and British spelling:

re*fer* : referred
oc*cur* : occurring

Note, however, *reference* and *occurrence*.

1.3 With the change of tense from present to past we get the impression that cats are extinct (that is, they no longer exist), and also that the English language appears to be extinct too. (In such a state of affairs the pronoun 'we' would probably not be used, and one might read instead: 'but they did not call a man a "cat".'.)

1.4 The new passage should read as follows:

Cats are independent animals, but dogs are not. Dogs generally like company while cats often prefer to keep to themselves. Domestic cats still have a lot in common with their bigger sisters, the lion and the tiger, but most domestic dogs do not have much in common with their wild relative, the wolf. In ancient times, the cat was a goddess while the dog was a worker, protecting sheep and the home. It is also an interesting fact that in English the cat is female, but the dog is not, being regarded as male. A male cat gets the special name 'tomcat' to show that he is not female, while the female dog gets the special name 'bitch' to show that she is not male.

Note: There is usually a comma in front of the conjunction *but*, and there may or may not be one in front of *while*, depending on how sharp the comparison is.

1.5 Punctuation work: First stage

In the version of the text below, ordinary word-stress is shown by underlining the stressed syllables, while sentence-stress (or tonic stress, as it is sometimes called) is shown by printing certain stressed syllables in capital letters. On these syllables the tone of the sentence changes, up or down, depending on the requirements of intonation. (The version here is only *one* of a large number of possible good ways of reading the text.)

CATS are indePENdent animals. They are doMEStic animals, like dogs, but they are not so comPLEtely domestic as dogs. They like to keep SOME secrets. They have their own private LIVES. The doMEStic cat is very much a hunter and a wanderer like her BIGger sisters, the LIon and the TIger. The ancient eGYptians were probably the FIRST people to keep cats, but they did not keep them as PETS. The cat was a GOD in ancient Egypt, or, more correctly, a GODDess. It is an interesting fact that people USUAlly refer to cats as female. A MALE cat gets a special name to show that he is NOT female. He is a 'TOMcat'. In the ENGlish language, a woman is called a 'CAT' if she says unkind things about other WOmen, but we do not call a man a 'cat' if he says unkind things about other MEN. If a MAN is not very nice, we call him a 'DOG' or a 'RAT'.

Punctuation work: Second stage

Check the punctuation of the first passage against the appropriate part of the passage about cats. The second passage should look as follows:

A friend of mine has a cat called Cleopatra. This cat sometimes goes away for weeks, and no one sees her or knows where she is. Occasionally, however, my friend finds her sitting on a wall in the moonlight, miles from home. Cleopatra comes down from the wall, rubs herself against my friend to say 'hullo', then walks away again. She comes back about a week later, quite happy, in her own good time. Cleopatra is independent. She certainly lives with my friend, but she does not in any sense belong to him.

1.6
a. wanderers
b. manlike/man-like
c. hostess
d. Developing
e. learned
f. murderer
g. dogged; doglike/dog-like
h. planner
i. ratlike/rat-like
j. skilled, worker

1.7
a. The dog generally likes company.
b. The lion must kill in order to live.
c. The tiger is a powerful animal.
d. The rose is a beautiful flower.
e. In ancient Egypt, the cat was a goddess.
f. The square is a geometrical figure.
g. The tree is important in our lives.
h. The elephant is a very large animal.
i. He has been studying tigers and their habits.
j. It is easier to grow roses in some climates than in others.
k. Kangaroos are found in Australia, but jaguars are native to Central and South America.
l. Cats were certainly considered divine in ancient Egypt.
m. Wolves and hyenas are wild animals while dogs are domestic animals.
n. Tigers and lions are very large, but domestic cats are relatively small.
o. Although some people prefer roses, I prefer tulips and daffodils because they are spring flowers.
p. Circles and triangles are common figures in geometry.
q. the oak and the elm are trees which grow slowly.
r. Rats are animals that carry disease.
s. Dogs are often called man's best friend(s).

t. Many people regard oak trees as symbols of strength/as a symbol of strength.
u. The dog is a popular animal in English-speaking countries, but men are still called 'dogs' if they are not nice to people/but a man is still called a dog if he is not nice to people.
v. The ancient Greeks did not have a high opinion of dogs.
w. The deer is not usually a domestic animal.
x. Sheep and goats are similar, but they are not members of the same species.
y. (1) X; (2) X; (3) X; (4) X; (5) The; (6) a; (7) a; (8) the; (9) the;
z. (1) The; (2) an; (3) a; (4) the; (5) the; (6) X; (7) X; (8) X; (9) the; (10) the

1.8   Animal Names

In the English language, the names of animals are often used to describe people. If a man is not very nice, some people might call him a 'rat'. If he is quiet, dull and not very brave, they might call him a 'mouse'. If he tries to trick other people, they might call him a 'fox'. We do this because we think that some kinds of animals and some kinds of people share the same qualities.

In English, we sometimes use adjectives taken from the names of animals to describe other things. We say, for example, that something is 'fishy' if we feel that it has a bad smell or is suspicious in some way. We sometimes say that a woman is 'catty' if she says unkind things about other women. People are 'foxy' if they are always trying to trick other people. Decriptions that use animal names are usually not compliments.

1.9   People's Attitudes to Animals

People's attitudes to animals can be very different in different parts of the world. In some places, for example, dogs are popular as domestic pets, but in others they are never allowed inside the house. They are kept outside, to help with sheep or to guard property. In India, the cow is a sacred animal and is never killed or eaten, while in the western world cattle are kept to provide milk and meat, and people have no special feelings about them.

In many languages, names for animals are used to describe people. These names serve to express our strong opinions about both animals and human beings and generally OR in general they are not complimentary. Nobody usually enjoys being compared to OR with an animal. In modern English, no woman wants to be compared to OR with a cat or a cow, and no man wants to be called a 'dog' or a 'rat'.

From the point of view of sciences like zoology OR a science like zoology, of course, these comparisons have no meaning. They relate instead to our cultural and emotional attitudes, and therefore interest people who study the human mind.

1.10 The correct form of the text on horses and cows is:

Horses are useful animals, but they are not more useful than cows. It is easier to ride a horse than a cow, but it is easier to milk a cow than a horse. Cows are generally regarded as female OR as females, and the male gets the special name 'bull' to show that he is not female. Horses, however, are generally regarded as male OR as males, the female getting the special name 'mare' to show that she is not male. We can, however, call the OR a male horse a 'stallion', but there is no special name, in the English language at least, for a female cow.

UNIT 2

2.1 a. **T**
 b. **T**
 c. **F:** His father used to take things to sell in the town.
 d. **T**
 e. **F:** The bus turned many corners.
 f. **F:** The bus took four hours to get from its starting place to the plain.
 g. **F:** The town was built on a plain.
 h. **T**

2.2 a. no change: *ways*
 b. change: *lazier, laziest, lazily*
 c. no change: *monkeys*
 d. change: *parties*
 e. no change: *days* (**Note** *daily*)
 f. change: *earlier, earliest*
 g. change: *friendlier, friendliest*
 h. X
 i. no change: *donkeys*
 j. change: *rockier, rockiest*
 k. X
 l. change: *skies*
 m. change: *lonelier, loneliest*
 n. change: *worried, worrier*
 o. change: *necessarily*
 p. normally no change, but **note** the special legal plurals *moneys/monies* (not normally used)

If you have any doubts about how to spell words like these, study the following rules:

1 Normally, a noun, adjective or verb ending in a consonant and a *y* will change the *y* into *i* when a suffix is added:

party : parties   lazy : lazily
easy : easier   carry : carried

2 If, however, the word ends in a vowel followed by *y*, the *y* is not changed:

journey : journeys/journeyed
essay : essays

3 Additionally, if the suffix begins with an *i*, there is no change:

carry : carrying
hurry : hurrying

2.3 Analysis and synthesis: First stage

(FV: finite verb   C: conjunction
ST: sentence type)

 1 FV: was   C: *none*   ST: simple
 2 FV: was, was, waited   C: and, where
    C: compound-complex
 3 FV: was   C: *none*   ST: simple
 4 FV: have, is   C: and   ST: compound
 5 FV: used to take, carried   C: and
    ST: compound
 6 FV: remember, was, took   C: how,
    when   ST: complex
 7 FV: was, was   C: and   ST: compound
 8 FV: was, stopped   C: and
    ST: compound
 9 FV: rolled, turned, got   C: and, until
    ST: compound-complex
10 FV: took   C: *none*   ST: simple
11 FV: saw   C: *none*   ST: simple
12 FV: were working   C: *none*   ST: simple
13 FV: waved, passed, waved back   C: as,
    and   ST: compound-complex
14 FV: came   C: *none*   ST: simple
15 FV: was, had, were   C: but, than
    ST: compound

Analysis and synthesis: Second stage

a. At that time there was no railway, but there is now.
b. There was a bus three times a week and it was necessary to walk a few kilometres to the bus station.
c. Cats are independent animals and have their own private lives.
d. Cats are not completely domestic, because they still like to hunt and wander about.
e. There was a train every day, but it was necessary for us to walk a few miles to the station, because we lived out of town.
f. I was very young at the time and got very excited when he asked me to go with him.
g. It is an interesting fact that people usually refer to cats as female.
h. Some people spoke to us as we were walking past the shops, because they wanted to sell us things.
i. It is true that buses go regularly to all the villages and bring people to work in the city.
j. Women are called 'cats' if they say unkind things about other women, but men are not called 'cats' if they say unkind things about other men.
k. When my father went to town he sold things, because he often needed money to buy new tools and materials.
l. Although my father lived in a village and did not like big towns, he often had to go to the nearest city, where he could sell his goods.

Analysis and synthesis: Third stage

In those days, it was necessary to travel on foot or on horseback, because there were no trains, buses or cars in that part of the country. I remember when I was about nine years old and my father took me with him down the mountain to the big town on the plain. We travelled all day, until we came to a small inn on the edge of the town, where my father usually stayed. We had a good meal and slept soundly that night, or, at least, I did, because I was so tired. In the morning, early, my father took me with him to the market and I learned a lot by watching him bargaining.

Note   Commas can be omitted from around 'at least' and 'early', if the writer feels that there is a danger of too many commas.

2.4 Punctuation work: First stage Nil

Punctuation work: Second stage

Cats are independent animals. Dogs, however, are not. Dogs generally like to be part of the family, while cats like to keep some secrets of their own. Domestic cats still have a lot in common with their bigger sisters, the lion and the tiger, but most domestic dogs do not have much in common with their wild relative, the wolf. In ancient times, the cat was a goddess, but the dog was a worker, protecting sheep and the home.

Punctuation work: Third stage

At that time, people were travelling every day from our village to the big city. They did this because there was no work for them in the village, but most people could find some kind of work in the city. I remember very clearly the day when I first went to the city to look for a job. I tried to look brave, but inside me I was feeling pretty nervous. I walked through the city all day, going to many places. I tried shops, hotels, factories, a government office, the bus station and the railway station, but there were no jobs. I was unlucky that day.

2.5

1 the	8 the	15 a	22 the
2 the	9 a	16 X	23 X
3 the	10 the	17 X	24 a
4 an	11 a	18 a	25 an
5 a	12 the	19 the	26 a
6 a	13 a	20 X	27 the
7 a	14 A	21 X	28 X

2.6

a.	monthly	f.	stony
b.	sandy	g.	saintly
c.	powdery	h.	salty
d.	yearly	i.	foggy
e.	brotherly	j.	quarterly

2.7 ## Scotland

I remember how pleased I was when my father took me to Fort William for the first time. I was about twelve years old at the time and had never been to the Scottish Highlands before. We travelled by bus from Glasgow. The journey began at nine o'clock in the

morning and took several hours. It was very interesting because the bus passed through such beautiful country. On the way I saw mountains, forests, rivers and 'lochs', which is the Scottish name for lakes. When at last we reached Fort William I was ready for a good lunch and then an afternoon exploring the town.

France

I remember how excited I was when my mother took me to Paris for my first visit. I was not more than eleven then. We went there by express train from Bordeaux. The train left at eight in the morning and the journey lasted several hours. It was interesting because I was able to see many places that I had never seen before. We had a meal on the train and talked to several people who lived and worked in Paris OR who were living and working in Paris. When at length we got there I felt rather small in such a big city and was a little worried by all the traffic. It was, however, a memorable trip.

2.8 Ten corrections as follows:

1 In the late 19th century ...
2 ... in Central Africa.
3 ... he journeyed ...
4 ... is now called ...
5 A hundred years later ...
6 ... soldiers and scientists ...
7 About Stanley, the leader ...
8 ... expedition, Colonel John Snell, said:
9 ... don't ...
10 ... to get through.'

UNIT 3

3.1 a. **F**: He was a Greek hero.
 b. **T**
 c. **T**
 d. **F**: It was a warship that guarded the supply lines.
 e. **T**
 f. **F**: The magazine blew up, blowing a hole in the bows.
 g. **T**
 h. **T**

3.2 a. does OR did
 b. dying
 c. written
 d. taken
 e. destruction
 f. terrific **OR** terrible
 g. description
 h. firing
 i. icy
 j. wintry
 k. driven
 l. blown

3.3 a. There were many dogs that guarded the camp.
 b. I saw several houses that were for sale.
 c. He wrote a book that describes war in the Atlantic.
 d. In those days, there were a lot of ships that sailed back and forth between the islands.
 e. He made many journeys that took him to the farthest corners of the earth.
 f. The dogs that/which guarded the camp were dangerous.
 g. The book that/which describes the war is in the library.
 h. The letters that/which must be posted today are on the table.
 i. The houses that/which must be sold soon are in the village.
 j. The story that/which was written by Alistair Maclean describes a ship called the *Ulysses*.
 k. This is the work (which/that) he used to do.
 l. She works in the library (which/that) I showed you yesterday.
 m. That is the ship (which/that) he mentioned last night.
 n. This is that cat (which/that) my friend calls Cleopatra.
 o. They showed us the map (which/that) he used when he travelled down the Zaire river.
 p. This is the book about which I was telling you/which I was telling you about/that I was telling you about/I was telling you about.
 q. That is the village to which he goes back every year/which he goes back to every year/that he goes back to every year/he goes back to every year.
 r. The *Ulysses* was a warship to which many terrible things happened/which many terrible things happened to/(that) many terrible things happened to.
 s. The animals to which he referred in his books were very interesting/which he referred to in his books .../(that) he referred to in his books ...
 t. The journey from which he has just returned was long and difficult/which he has just returned from was .../(that) he has just returned from was ...

3.4 1 FV: was, is C: but ST: compound
 2 FV: is, does ... have D: and ST: compound
 3 FV: like, is C: if ST: complex
 4 FV: takes (place), centres, guarded C: and, that ST: compound-complex
 5 FV: suggests, is C: that ST: complex
 6 FV: describes, die C: how ST: complex
 7 FV: describes, went on C: how ST: complex
 8 FV: blew up, rushed in C: so that ST: complex
 9 FV: drove ... onward/downward, took C: and ST: compound

The sentences of the passage in tabular form
are as follows:

first statements	connecting words	second statements
The original Ulysses was an ancient Greek hero.	but	Maclean's Ulysses is a ship.
The story entitled *HMS Ulysses* is about men, ships and war in the awful conditions of the North Atlantic and Arctic.	and	(It) does not have a happy ending.
If you like happy endings. . . .	then	This is just not the book for you.
The action takes place during the Second World War.	and	(It) centres on the *Ulysses*, just one ship among the many ships . . .
	that	guarded the Allied supply lines in the North Atlantic.
Its story suggests . . .	that	War is pointless and wasteful, destroying good men and good ships to no purpose.
Maclean describes . . .	how	The *Ulysses* and her sailors die in the ice, fire and water at the top of the world, during a terrible northern winter.
At the end of the book, he describes . . .	how	The warship went on through terrific seas, covered with ice and badly damaged, but still moving at high speed.
Then her magazine blew up, blowing a great hole in her bows.	so that	The seas rushed in.
She drove herself onward and downward into the rolling waters, 'to the black floor of the Arctic', her great engines still turning.	and	(She) took every man with her.

3.5 a. There were many dogs guarding the camp.
   b. He read the book describing war in the North Atlantic.
   c. She read an account showing how the ship sank.
   d. There are not very many places providing this kind of information.
   e. There were a lot of ships needing urgent help.
   f. The dogs guarding the camp were dangerous.
   g. The book describing the war fully is in the library.
   h. Offices providing this kind of help are not common.
   i. Aircraft flying across the Atlantic need plenty of fuel.
   j. Work providing good pay and conditions is not always easy to find.

k. The camp guarded by the dogs was never attacked.

l. Aircraft provided with plenty of fuel fly across the Atlantic every day.

m. Books written by people like Alistair Maclean are usually exciting to read.

n. It is not pleasant to read about ships or cities destroyed as a result of war.

o. Maclean's book, described as one of the most exciting sea stories ever written, is in our local library.

3.6 Passage 1

People love stories. Children like listening to stories at bedtime, and adults like reading them or watching them on television. There is a large market in storybooks almost everywhere in the world, thousands of stories for all tastes, but ultimately only a few basic plots OR but, ultimately, only a few basic plots. New books and films tell the world's old stories in endless new ways. *HMS Ulysses*, for example, is the old theme of men fighting both natural and human enemies. Even when such men are defeated they have in a sense OR defeated, they have in a sense OR they have, in a sense, still won their battles, because we do not forget them. Writers like Alistair Maclean also take old names like 'Ulysses', names which have their own special power, and use them in new ways, giving them fresh significance.

Passage 2

In the late 19th century, an American journalist called Henry Stanley travelled widely in Central Africa. Wherever he went, he took with him a small wooden boat that could be taken to pieces, and on this boat he journeyed down the great river then called the Congo but nowadays known as the Zaire. A hundred years later, in early 1975, a group of British soldiers and scientists repeated Stanley's historic journey, using modern equipment and inflatable boats with engines. This expedition was led by Colonel

John Snell, a great admirer of Stanley. The group did not find the trip easy, and Snell wondered how on earth Stanley had managed it at all. They were chased by animals, fell sick with fever, and found the river currents dangerous. Snell commented afterwards that sometimes OR that, sometimes, the river seemed alive, its great whirlpools often threatening to swallow them up.

Note that in these various passages for punctuation you are free to make your own paragraph divisions and, by and large, to punctuate differently from the models given here – as long as you can defend your decisions.

3.7 a. hopeless
b. wastefully
c. endless
d. sleeveless
e. purposefully
f. meaningless
g. harmful
h. valueless
i. powerful, powerless

3.8 (1) story
(2) hour
(3) doing
(4) both
(5) enemies
(6) worse
(7) forget
(8) least
(9) way
(10) comfort

3.9 The Narrow Escape

The Northern Queen was sailing in the Arctic Ocean as part of a scientific survey. She was working farther north than the other two ships in her group. It was now late in the year and there was still a great deal of work to be done. The captain therefore took a risk. He delayed as long as possible in the area, although winter ice was beginning to form. He delayed too long, however, as ice began to surround OR began surrounding the ship. Soon there was no way out in any direction. After several more days, the Northern Queen was completely trapped. The captain sent an urgent radio message OR urgent radio messages for help, because there was now a real danger that the weight of ice would crush the ship. Rescue reached them by air just in time, however, saving the crew although the unfortunate vessel could not be saved OR although, unfortunately, the vessel could not be saved.

UNIT 4

4.1   a. F: It was Shahriyar.
   b. F: He did not like being deceived by women.
   c. F: She did not know it for sure, and she planned to avoid being executed.
   d. T
   e. T
   f. F: We do not know this. We are told that they did.
   g. F: She lived on because the king began to love her.
   h. T

4.2   Nil

3.10   The passage is edited with the number of faults per line indicated in the lefthand margin.

X   Every species of animal has its own character. Cats, for example,
XX   are more independent than dogs and have their own private lives,
X   while dogs are, on the whole, more domestic and useful than cats.
X   Horses, in the past, have been even more useful to the human race
XXX   than dogs, but it is probably true to say that, of all animals, the cow is the
X   most valuable. The cow provides a whole range of foodstuffs: milk,
X   butter, cheese, yoghurt and cream, and many people also eat its
XX   meat. In India, however, most people do not eat beef and will do
X   anything to avoid killing cows.

It is difficult to imagine the wild ancestors of many of our
X   domestic animals. We can, however, look at the tiger to see what a large wild cat is like and at the wolf to see what the original
X   ancestral form of a spaniel or a poodle really was. The human race
X   today no longer lives closely associated with animal life, and many
XXX   of us come close to real wild creatures only when we go to a zoo[1],
XX   unless of course we consider that some human beings are wild rather
X   than domestic.[2] If that is true, then we often meet wild creatures
X   driving cars dangerously or causing other kinds of trouble.

[1] OR to the zoo. OR to zoos.
[2] OR BETTER are more wild than domestic

4.3 a. Cats are domestic animals. They are not, however, so completely domestic as dogs/ However, they are not so completely domestic as dogs.

Cats are domestic animals. Still, they are ...

Cats are domestic animals. Even so, they are ...

Cats are domestic animals, but even so they are ...

Cats are domestic animals. They are nevertheless not so completely domestic as dogs.

Although/Though cats are domestic animals, they ...

Even though cats are ...

    b. The ancient Egyptians were the first people to keep cats. They did not, however, keep them as pets./However, they did not keep them as pets.

The ancient Egyptians were the first people to keep cats. Still, they ... Even so, they ...

The ancient. ... to keep cats, but even so they ...

The ancient Egyptians were the first people to keep cats. They nevertheless did not .../Nevertheless, they did not ...

Although/Though the ancient Egyptians ...

    c. Horses are useful animals. They are not, however, as useful as cows./However, they are not as useful as cows.

Horses are useful animals. Still, they ... Even so, they ...

Horses are useful animals, but even so they ...

Horses are useful animals. They are nevertheless not as useful as cows./ Nevertheless, they are not as useful as cows.

Although/Though horses are useful animals, they ...

Even though horses are useful animals, they ...

    d. It was not a big town. To the child, however, it seemed to have more houses than there were stars in the sky./ However, to the child it seemed to have ...

It was not a big town. Still, to the child ... Even so, to the child ...

It was not a big town, but even so, to the child, it seemed to have more houses than there were stars in the sky.

It was not a big town. To the child it nevertheless seemed .../Nevertheless, to the child it seemed .. Although/Though it was not a big town, to the child ...

Even though it was not a big town, to the child ...

    e. The original Ulysses was an ancient Greek hero. Maclean's Ulysses, however, is a ship./However, Maclean's Ulysses is a ship.

The original Ulysses was an ancient Greek hero. Still, Maclean's ... Even so, Maclean's ...

The original ... Greek hero, but even so Maclean's ...

The original Ulysses was an ancient Greek hero. Maclean's Ulysses is, nevertheless, a ship./Nevertheless, Maclean's ...

Although/Though the original Ulysses ...

Even though the original Ulysses ...

4.4 a. The queen wanted to live. She therefore told endless stories./Therefore she told endless stories./She consequently told .../Consequently, she told ...

    b. She expected to meet him in town at 12 o'clock. She therefore left home at 11.30./Therefore she left .../She consequently left .../Consequently, she left ...

    c. He did not want to be sent away. He therefore tried even harder to please them./Therefore he tried .../He consequently tried .../Consequently, he tried ...

    d. The sailors did not want to be trapped by the ice. They therefore sent urgent radio messages for help./Therefore they sent

.../They consequently sent .../
Consequently, they sent ...

e. The travellers decided that it would be easier to reach their destination by river than by road. They therefore began looking for someone with a suitable boat./Therefore they began .../They consequently began ... Consequently, they began ...

f. Because the queen wanted to live, she told endless stories./The queen told endless stories because she wanted to live.

g. Because she expected to meet him in town at 12 o'clock, she left home at 11.30./She left home at 11.30 because she expected to meet him in town at 12 o'clock.

h. Because he did not want to be sent away, he tried even harder to please them./He tried even harder to please them because he did not want to be sent away.

i. Because the sailors did not want to be trapped by the ice, they sent urgent radio messages for help./The sailors sent urgent radio messages for help because they did not want to be trapped by the ice.

j. Because the travellers decided that it would be easier to reach their destination by river than by road, they began looking for someone with a suitable boat./The travellers began looking for someone with a suitable boat because they decided that ...

k. The queen told endless stories, so that she would not be executed./So that she would not be executed, the queen told endless stories.
The queen told endless stories to make sure that she was not OR that she would not be executed./To make sure that she was not OR that she would not be executed, the queen told endless stories.
The queen told endless stories in order that she would not be executed./In order that she would not be executed, the queen told endless stories.

l. He took a taxi so that he would get to the station on time./So that he would get to the station on time, he took a taxi.
He took a taxi to make sure that he got OR that he would get to the station on time./To make sure that he got OR that he would get to the station on time, he took a taxi.
He took a taxi in order that he would get to the station on time./In order that he would get to the station on time, he took a taxi.

m. She worked very hard, so that she would not lose her job. So that she would not lose her job, she worked very hard.
She worked very hard to make sure that she did not OR that she would not lose her job./To make sure that she did not OR that she would not lose her job, she worked very hard.
She worked very hard in order that she would not lose her job./In order that she would not lose her job, she worked very hard.

n. They did the work at night as well as during the day, so that they would/could finish it quickly./So that they would/could finish it quickly, they did ...
They did the work at night as well as during the day to make sure that they finished it OR that they would/could finish it quickly./To make sure that they finished OR that they would/could finish it quickly, they did the work ...
They did the work at night as well as during the day in order that they would/could finish it quickly./In order that they would/could finish it quickly, they did the work at night as well as during the day.

o. The sailors sent urgent radio messages for help, so that they would not be trapped by the ice./So that they would not be trapped by the ice, the sailors ...
The sailors sent urgent radio messages for help to make sure that they were not OR that they would not be trapped by the ice./To make sure that they were not OR that they would not be trapped by

the ice, the sailors … The sailors sent urgent radio messages for help in order that they would not be trapped by the ice./In order that they would not be trapped by the ice, the sailors …

4.5 a. Cats are domestic animals, like dogs, but they are not so completely domestic as dogs.

b. The cat was a god in ancient Egypt, or, more correctly, a goddess.

c. Cleopatra, my friend's cat, occasionally goes away for weeks and no one knows where she is. Sometimes, however, my friend finds her sitting on a wall in the moonlight, miles from home.

d. If a woman behaves badly, especially towards other women, she is called a 'cat'.

e. We had a good meal, and slept soundly that night, or at least I did, because I was tired OR that night, or, at least, I did, because I was tired.

f. When at length we got there OR When, at length, we got there, I felt rather small in such a big city as Paris, and was a little worried by all the traffic. It was, however, a memorable trip.

g. Writers like Alistair Maclean take old names like 'Ulysses' – names which have their own special power – and use them in new ways.

h. A hundred years later, in early 1975, a group of British soldiers and scientists repeated Stanley's journey down the Zaire, one of Africa's greatest rivers, travelling in inflatable boats with engines.

i. Every species of animal has its own character. Cats, for example, are more independent than dogs, and have their own private lives, while dogs are on the whole OR are, on the whole, more domestic and useful than cats. Horses in the past have been OR Horses, in the past, have been even more useful to the human race than dogs, but it is probably true to say that of all animals OR that, of all animals, the cow has been and still is OR the cow has been – and still is – the most valuable.

j. Long ago, according to The Thousand and One Nights, there lived in the land of China a tailor called Mustafa. He was very poor and had few possessions, but he did have a son called Aladdin. Mustafa wanted Aladdin to learn how to make clothes, so that he could be useful in the tailor's shop, but Aladdin did not want to. All he wanted to do was to play games in the street with other boys. Then his father fell ill and died, leaving his poor widow to look after everything. Sometimes she asked OR Sometimes, she asked her useless son to help her, but he never did. It is interesting that fate should have given to that most unhelpful child a wonderful lamp that granted him everything he could wish for. Life is hardly fair.

4.6 (1) known
(2) has
(3) such
(4) purely
(5) plan
(6) are
(7) however
(8) pouring
(9) usually
(10) managing

4.7 a. independent
b. improbable
c. uninteresting
d. non-medical
e. unguarded
f. unforgettable
g. undamaged
h. insufficient
i. impractical
j. invisible

4.8 The Discontented Frogs

There was a time, in ancient Athens, when the people were unhappy with their king, Peisistratos OR with King Peisistratos.

He had not done very much OR He did not do very much, and they consequently wanted a better and more active sort of king. A traveller called Aesop told them that there was once OR there had once been a community of frogs that (had) felt the same way. The Frogs had been just as unhappy as the Athenians. At first they were OR they had been in an even worse situation, because they had no king at all. They therefore asked the great god Zeus to give them one.

Zeus thought about it and said that, in his opinion, the Frogs were stupid. They were OR would be better off without a king. In order to please them, however, he threw a large log of wood into the pool where they lived, and said that it would make them a very fine king indeed.

King Log made a great splash when he arrived. At first OR At first, the Frogs were frightened of their new ruler and hid from him. However, they soon got used to him, and saw that he only made one big splash. They therefore grew bold and OR grew bold, and began to jump OR began jumping all over their new king, showing no respect at all. Their opinion of the great god Zeus was not very high either OR high, either. They told him to take this useless king away and give them a proper king with some life in him instead.

Zeus was annoyed at OR by their stupidity. Their demand would, however, be met, for he sent them a tall, hungry, sharp-eyed stork. When King Stork arrived he made no splash – but he was full of life.

He was fond of frogs – and soon he was full of them too.

4.9 The Powerful Pigs

The passage is edited with the number of faults per line indicated in the lefthand margin.

X	There was once a farmer who did not do his work very well and (who)
X	was cruel to his animals. It is not surprising, therefore, that the
	animals hated him and that they met secretly in order to plan a
XX	revolution. The pigs led the revolution and the other animals followed.
	The animals chased the bad farmer out and set up a special new
XXX	form of government where all the animals were to be equal. No one
XX	would walk on two legs like the farmer, and no one would live in
	the frightening farmhouse.
XX	Things went quite well for a time after that. The pigs were the
XXX	cleverest animals on the farm and were good leaders. They told the
XX	other animals what to do and began to enjoy giving orders. They
XX	even trained the young dogs as a kind of police force, to make sure
X	that the rest of the animals did exactly as they were ordered.[1] Some
X	pigs were not entirely happy about this new way of doing things,[2]
	however. They had originally believed strongly in a true and equal
XX	revolution. These pigs were not left in peace. They were chased out
X	like the farmer, and some were even killed. Meanwhile, the other
XX	pigs moved into the farmhouse, which was clearly the best place
	for leaders to live. Life for most of the animals was not much better
X	now then it had been before the revolution – but at least the new

> X   masters did not walk on two legs. In fact, the animals worked
> X   harder than ever and, though life was better for the pigs, it was not
> better for the majority of the inhabitants of Animal Farm. The pigs
> had an explanation for this,[3] however. They agreed that all animals
> X   were equal, but they insisted that some animals were more equal than
> others.

[1] New paragraph   [2] OR Some pigs, however, were . . .   [3] OR The pigs, however, had . . .

UNIT 5

5.1 **1** a. **T**
           b. **T**
           c. **F**: The accident happened on the old road.
           d. **T**
           e. **F**: The third car was travelling too fast.
           f. **F**: The third car went off the road.
           g. **T**
           h. **T**
           i. **F**: Nothing happened to the people in the second car.
           j. **F**: The boy's father was not in the car, although his mother was.

    2 a. the first sentence of the first paragraph
           b. the second sentence of the first paragraph
           c. *The* automobile (line 2)
           d. If people . . . could not otherwise be done. (lines 4–7)
           e. the beginning of the second paragraph
           f. 1 making possible, etc (line 5)
              2 telling everybody (line 18)
           g. 'super-highway' (line 14)
           h. lines 8–9 and line 25
           i. lines 11, 27 and 30
           j. – and dangerous – (line 13)
           k. the beginning of the fourth paragraph
           l. line 12
           m. . . . although traffic does often come off the motorway into the town faster . . . (lines 15–16)
           n. I think the driver . . . (lines 23–24)
           o. 1 It did. (line 25)
              2 They never got to the shops. (lines 34–35)

5.2 **Nil**

5.3

analysis	participial
analytical	participle
article	passage
comma	period
communicate	phrase
communication	plural
compare	positive
comparison	prefix
composition	pronoun
comprehension	punctuation
concession	quotation
conditional	reason
conjunction	reference
connection	relation
consequence	relative
consonant	result
control	sentence
definite	single
dialogue	singular
double	speech
edit	spelling
grammar	structure
grammatical	style
model	suffix
parenthesis	synthesis
parenthetical	synthetic

tense	vocabulary
test	vocal
text	voice
unit	vowel

5.4

(1) Although	(11) that/which
(2) If	(12) where
(3) because	(13) that/which
(4) that/which	(14) and
(5) when	(15) Although
(6) where	(16) and
(7) and	(17) when
(8) because/when	(18) what
(9) who	(19) that
(10) when	(20) when

5.5

(1) a	(10) The	(18) the
(2) the	(11) the	(19) the
(3) the	(12) the	(20) the
(4) the	(13) X	(21) X
(5) a	(14) the	(22) X
(6) the	(15) X	(23) X
(7) the	(16) The	(24) The
(8) the	(17) the	(25) the
(9) a		

5.6 Gulliver's Travels

The book called *Gulliver's Travels* is, in many ways, similar to *The Thousand and One Nights* and *Aesop's Fables*, because it uses strange situations in faraway lands and also makes humorous comments on human nature. It is, therefore, (OR omit commas) a fantasy with a practical purpose.

Essentially, the book describes what happens to Gulliver when he goes on sea voyages. (OR in the past tense, although generally the present is preferred when describing events in books) On the first occasion, his ship is wrecked and he finds himself in Lilliput, the land of little people. Later, he goes by accident to the land of giants, called Brobdingnag. (OR in each case 'a land', if one does not wish to be too specific) On still another occasion, he has an adventure OR adventures in the/a land of talking horses.

In fact, all these little people, giants and horses represent human beings. The author, Jonathan Swift, liked writing about people, politics and society, and suggested that, from a certain point of view, important problems in a country might appear very small and unimportant. Swift also meant that some people have small minds, and need to realize just how insignificant they are in the universe. He suggested that some horses' minds are perhaps better than some people's, or, at least, it is interesting to hear intelligent speech come/coming from a horse. (OR no commas around 'at least', and possibly past tense throughout the sentence)

Although today *Gulliver's Travels* is read mainly for the sake of the/its stories, originally Swift wrote it in order to shock people – and in this he succeeded.

UNIT 6

6.1

a. F: She did not know this.
b. F: He had rented the house.
c. F: She wanted her husband to call on Mr Bingley first.
d. F: Mr Bennet had not planned to call on Mr Bingley.
e. T
f. T
g. F: He possibly sympathized with Mr Bingley.
h. T

6.2 Nil

6.3

a. Mrs Bennet said (that) a new young man had just come to Netherfield Park.

b. She added (that) his name was Bingley and (that) he came from the north.

c. She suggested (that) her husband/Mr Bennet should call on him the next day. (**Note** that, very formally, we can also say: 'She suggested that her husband call on him the next day.')

d. Mr Bennet said cautiously (that) he had no plan to do so.

e. She said firmly (that) he would make a wonderful match for one of the girls.

f. He suggested (that) she should make a list of the good qualities of each girl and (that) he could (then) send it to the young man.

g. She said angrily (that) she would (*informally* she'd) do nothing of the kind. (**Note** that exclamation and question marks belonging with direct speech are not carried over into the indirect report.)

h. Her husband said (that) Elizabeth was the best.

i. She answered that he always preferred Elizabether. (**Note** that it is still possible to omit the *that* in this sentence, but that the result is awkward and suggests direct speech when said aloud.)

j. He replied with a smile that he did not/ didn't.

6.4   Passage 1

'Well, my dear, did you call on Mr Bingley?' asked Mrs Bennet excitedly.

'Yes, I did,' he replied, smiling.

'What happened?'

'Well, you may be glad to know that we shall all be seeing this young gentleman quite soon.'

'When? Where? What on earth do you mean?'

Mr Bennet laughed, pleased at his wife's response.

'It is simple, my dear,' he answered. 'He has been invited to the ball and has agreed to go OR to the ball, and has agreed to go. He will therefore have every opportunity not only to see but also to dance with every one of our daughters if he has a mind to do so.'

Passage 2

Pride and Prejudice is probably the most famous of Jane Austen's six novels about life, love and marriage among the middle classes of early 19th-century England. The other novels are *Sense and Sensibility*, *Emma*, *Mansfield Park*, *Persuasion*, and *Northanger Abbey*. Her style of writing mixes realism and romance in a way that was quite revolutionary at the time. She knew the society that she described, and took care not to move beyond it into subjects and places of which she had no personal knowledge and experience.

It was unusual at that time for 'well-bred' ladies to write, publish and earn money from books, and she therefore did not allow her name to appear on any of her books. Sir Walter Scott, in the *Quarterly Review* of March 1816, praised this 'nameless author' as a master of 'the modern novel'.

Jane Austen died the following year, at the age of 42, and it was only then that her authorship of the novels was revealed to the public by her brother Henry. She was indeed, as Scott suggested, a master of her craft, using ordinary everyday people and events in order to deal with the rich tragedy and comedy of human life.

Note   In this passage about Jane Austen I have organized the paragraphs in the way that seems most satisfactory to me. It is not the only possible way, nor is my use of commas in the passage the only possible way in which commas can be used.

Passage 3

Maria knew that he was coming. She put on her flowered dress with bows on the sleeves, combed her shiny black hair carefully and, having got ready earlier than usual, went every now and again to the window and looked up the road.

At last Abel came. He came on a bicycle which he put beside the gate.

'Is Maria at home?' he asked me nervously.

'Sure,' I said.

I ran inside to get her, although she already knew very well that he was there. It was all part of the game.

'I didn't expect to see you,' she lied, when she came out. 'I was getting dressed to go out.' But the way she smiled told Abel something different.

Much later, I saw Maria and Abel down by the river. I was with Ruth, and we hid among the bushes and watched with interest. Abel took Maria in his arms, gently, and gave her her first kiss.

'You can't call that a kiss at all!' said Ruth, but she had hardly said this when Abel kissed Maria again, and this time for so long that I wondered how they could hold their breath.

'That's what you can really call a kiss!' said Ruth, with respect.

6.5 a. (SR) I like the people, the town and the houses.

b. (IR) Who d'you think he'd seen?

c. (SR) Women usually like shopping, but men do not/(IR) but men don't.

d. (IR) I'll go if you'll go. OR I'll go if you will.

e. (SR) He went with her to get the money.

f. (SR) The men guarding the building fell asleep one by one.

g. (SR) Shahriyar, King of Persia, disliked women.

h. (IR) He's certainly the man we met yesterday.

i. (IR) She doesn't have to tell them they've won.

j. (SR) He found the second story just as interesting as the first.

k. *HMS Ulysses*, written by Alistair Maclean, describes the fate of a warship in Arctic waters.

l. The Frogs, eager to have an active and interesting king, asked the great god Zeus for his help.

m. *The Arabian Nights*, a collection of stories from the East, is set in ancient Iran.

n. The sailors, afraid in case *The Northern Queen* would be trapped in the ice, sent urgent radio messages for help.

o. *Aesop's Fables*, an ancient Greek collection of tales, uses insect and animal characters to describe human nature.

p. This temple, built by the Romans, is a perfect example of classical architecture.

q. *Animal Farm* by George Orwell is a book with a social and political purpose.

r. The fine old house, built by his family in the 18th century, has been their home ever since.

6.6 a. 2 It's possible he'll talk to Mr Bingley. 3 He may talk ... 4 He might talk ... 5 Perhaps he will OR he'll talk to Mr Bingley. 6 Maybe he will OR he'll talk ... 7 Perhaps he may OR might talk to Mr Bingley.

b. 1 It is possible that Elizabeth will need your help. 2 It's possible Elizabeth'll need your help. 4 Elizabeth might need your help. 5 Perhaps Elizabeth will OR Elizabeth'll need your help. 6 Maybe Elizabeth will OR Elizabeth'll ... 7 Perhaps Elizabeth may OR might need your help.

c. 1 It is possible that they will not see Mr Bennet at all. 2 It's possible they won't see ... 3 They may not see ... 4 Perhaps they will not OR won't see ... 5 Maybe they will not OR won't see ... 6 Perhaps they may OR might not see Mr Bennet at all.

d. 1 It is possible that they will leave soon. 2 It's possible they'll leave soon. 3 They may leave soon. 4 They might leave soon. 5 Perhaps they'll leave soon. 6 Maybe they will OR they'll leave soon. 7 Perhaps they may OR might leave soon.

e. 1 It is possible that I will OR shall go there next week. 2 It's possible I'll go there next week. 3 I may go there next week. 4 I might go... 5 Perhaps I will OR shall go there next week. 6 Maybe I will OR shall go there next week. 7 Perhaps I may OR might go there next week.

f. 1 It is possible that Mr Bingley will be able to come. 2 It's possible Mr Bingley'll be able to come. 3 Mr Bingley might be... 4 Perhaps Mr Bingley is able OR will be able to come. 5 Perhaps Mr Bingley can come. 6 Perhaps Mr Bingley could come. 7 Maybe Mr Bingley'll be able to come OR can come OR could come.

g. 1 It is possible that you will be able to find Elizabeth. 2 It's possible you'll be able to... 3 You may OR might be able to... 4 Perhaps you are able to find Elizabeth. 5 Perhaps you can... 6 Perhaps you could... 7 Maybe you'll be able OR you can OR you could... 8 Perhaps you may OR might be able to find Elizabeth.

h. 1 It is possible that we will OR shall all be able to go there together. 2 It's possible we'll all be able... 3 We may OR might all be able... 4 Perhaps we are all able OR will all be able... 5 Perhaps we can all... 6 Perhaps we could all... 7 Maybe we'll all be able to OR we could all go there together. 8 Perhaps we may OR might all be able to go there together.

i. 1 It is possible that Mrs Bennet will not be able to find husbands for all her daughters. 2 It's possible Mrs Bennet won't be able... 3 Mrs Bennet might not be able... 4 Perhaps Mrs Bennet is not able OR will not be able to... 5 Perhaps Mrs Bennet cannot find... 6 Perhaps Mrs Bennet could not find... 7 Maybe Mrs Bennet won't be able to find OR can't find OR couldn't find... **8 Perhaps Mrs Bennet may not OR might not be able to find husbands for all her daughters.**

j. 1 It is possible that they will not be able to go to the ball after all. 2 It's possible they won't be able... 3 They may not be able... **4 Perhaps they are not able to go OR will not be able to go... 5 Perhaps they cannot/can't go... 6 Perhaps they could not/couldn't go... 7 Maybe they won't be able to go OR can't go OR couldn't go...** 8 Perhaps they may OR might not be able to go to the ball after all.

k. 1 I do not know whether OR if Mr Bingley has a lot of money or not (*formal*). 2 I don't know whether OR if... (*informal*)

l. 1 We do not know whether OR if he will talk to us at the ball or not (*formal*). 2 We don't know... he'll talk to us... (*informal*).

m. 1 He is not sure whether OR if they can come or not (*formal*). 2 He's not sure OR He isn't sure... (*informal*).

n. Who knows whether OR if he went or not (*both*).

o. 1 They are not at all sure whether OR if she will find it or not (*formal*). 2 They're not sure OR They aren't sure at all... she'll find it or not (*informal*).

6.7 a. dramatic
b. commercially
c. unsympathetic
d. historic
e. unromantic
f. informal
g. nationally

h. idiomatically
i. energetic
j. cultural
k. industrially
l. systematic
m. undogmatically
n. confidentially
o. impersonal
p. irrational
q. illegal

6.8 Coming to See the Girl

In India, marriages are usually arranged by the parents. Most young people accept this state of affairs quite happily and assume that their parents can make good choices on their behalf. Sometimes, however, a girl or boy does not like the idea of an arranged marriage OR Sometimes, however, girls and boys do not like the idea of arranged marriages.

Shantha was like that. She felt she was a modern girl and not a subject for bargaining between families. She therefore hoped that her parents would not start looking for a husband for her.

One day, however, Shantha came home from college and saw mango leaves hanging over the front door. These leaves were OR are a sign welcoming people coming to see a girl.

'Oh no!' she thought. 'What shall I do?'

Meanwhile, Shantha's mother was thinking (that) her daughter would soon be leaving home OR would soon leave home in order to start a new life. Her mother was thinking of/about things to buy for the wedding and Shantha's new home. She was thinking (that) the boy's parents would ask if Shantha had a bank account to make the young couple's life more comfortable. The boy was tall and had a good job. His parents would ask for things like a bank account because it was OR it would be easy to find a wife for such a boy.

Shantha, meanwhile, was thinking (that) she was not something to bargain about, but was also frightened in case the visit proved OR would prove unsuccessful.

The doorbell rang.

The house suddenly seemed full of people talking and asking questions. People asked whether the daughter had returned yet from college.

Shantha's mother said: 'Yes. I'll go and get her.'

Shantha, who was waiting, said: 'Mother, am I all right?'

Her mother smiled and said, reassuringly: 'I know you'll be just perfect.'

UNIT 7

7.1
a. **F**: They played a kind of football, but not soccer.
b. **T**
c. **F**: He attended a game of football.
d. **T**
e. **T**
f. **T**
g. **T**
h. **T**
i. **F**: These games developed during Queen Victoria's reign, but not under her direct influence.
j. **T**

7.2
a. soldiers; necessary
b. popular; dangerous
c. permitted
d. dying
e. Curiously; extinction
f. private; nowhere; otherwise
g. evolve; special; style
h. enthusiastic; writing; violent; military
i. people; different; successfully
j. exciting; Association; beginning; appear

7.3

a.	2	n.	**Not relevant**
b.	1	o.	wouldn't
c.	4	p.	they'd
d.	1	q.	It'd
e.	2	r.	He'd
f.	3	s.	wouldn't
g.	1	t.	they'd: they'd
h.	4	u.	rushed; used to rush
i.	2	v.	was; would be
j.	4	w.	would go; used to go
k.	they'd	x.	saw; used to see
l.	pigs'd: they'd	y.	banned; would ban
m.	soldiers'd	z.	sat; used to sit

7.4

a. 1 **As given**
  2 It was a wonderful game, so . . .
  3 It was such a wonderful game (that) they . . .
  4 It was so wonderful a game that they . . .
  5 So wonderful a game was it that they . . .
  6 They really enjoyed it because it was such a wonderful game.

b. 1 **As given**
  2 It was a boring game, so . . .
  3 It was such a boring game (that) they . . .
  4 It was so boring a game that they . . .
  5 So boring a game was it that they . . .
  6 They did not enjoy it because it was such a boring game.

c. 1 **As given**
  2 It was an interesting sport, so . . .
  3 It was such an interesting sport (that) they . . .
  4 It was so interesting a sport that they . . .
  5 So interesting a sport was it that they . . .
  6 They liked watching it because it was such an interesting sport.

d. 1 **As given**
  2 This is a strange story, so . . .
  3 This is such a strange story (that) it . . .
  4 This is so strange a story that it . . .
  5 So strange a story is *it* that it . . . (**unusual**)
  6 It interests me very much because *it* is such a strange story.

e. 1 **As given**
  2 It is a beautiful country, so . . .
  3 It is such a beautiful country (that) I . . .
  4 It is so beautiful a country that I . . .
  5 So beautiful a country is it that I . . .
  6 I want to go there because it is such a beautiful country.

f. 1 **As given**
  2 He is a difficult man to talk to, so . . .
  3 He is such a difficult man to talk to (that) I . . .
  4 He is so difficult a man to talk to that I . . .
  5 So difficult a man to talk to is he that I . . . (**unusual**)
  6 I do not want to see him again because he is such a difficult man to talk to.

7.5

a. Because of/On account of/As a result of her beauty, she attracted many men.
b. Because of (etc) their excellence, we sold many of them.
c. On account of (etc) their newness, we find the machines hard to use.
d. As a result of (etc) her bad behaviour, they chose another candidate.
e. Because of his ability, we can give him work any time.
f. Because of her kindness, children like her very much.
g. As a result of their accuracy, people buy a lot of these watches./Because of the accuracy of these watches, people buy a lot of them.
h. On account of their friendliness, most people like them.
i. Because of her unhappiness, nothing seems to go right for her.
j. Because of the invasion (of the country), everybody had to fight.

Note

1 The commas in such sentences are optional, a matter of personal taste.

2 These sentences can also be reversed:
She attracted many men because of her beauty.
Children like her very much on account of her kindness.

3 The three phrases 'because of', 'on account of' and 'as a result of' are generally interchangeable, but for personal reasons of style some native users of English will prefer one particular phrase in certain situations rather than either or both of the others.

7.6 Punctuation work: First stage

a. The rich young men had nowhere to fish, hunt, ride or otherwise use up their energies; all they could do outside school hours was kick a ball in the schools' open spaces. It was out of such casual beginnings that the modern game of football emerged.

b. One public school, however, refused to co-operate, its delegates objecting to the new universal game. Rugby therefore left the new Association/association; it had its own plans, the result of which was a very different kind of game.

c. Since 1876, American football has been played by two teams of eleven players each. It is, however, very different from soccer; the ball is oval, like a rugby ball, and the players wear special padding and helmets to protect them from injuries. Although it is also played on an open field, it looks completely different from both British games.

d. Football developed rapidly in the 19th century; by Queen Victoria's time, for example, 17-year-old schoolboys were engaged in writing out its rules, taking the game with them to their universities, where they needed further rule-making so that people from different school backgrounds could play together. This

was how the world-famous Football Association began.

Note   One can argue in favour of or against the use of semi-colons in general, and the semi-colons here in particular. They can always, if you prefer it, be replaced by normal periods. It is also possible (and perhaps desirable) to argue about certain uses of commas in these sections. The important thing is that if you put a comma in a particular place you should know why you did it, and be able to justify your action afterwards.

Punctuation work: Second stage

Logical order: C.F.G.E.B.G.D.A.

Between 1870 and 1900, under the guidance of its remarkable secretary Charles Alcock, the F.A. changed soccer from a gentleman's weekend pastime into a great sporting spectacle. In 1871, Alcock founded the F.A. Challenge Cup, the first of the knockout competitions leading towards today's World Cup. In the same year, he took an English team to play in Scotland, and so created international football. In the 1880s, he faced the hard work of creating the Football League and established a world pattern for regular weekend competitions.

British people in Europe and South America organized football clubs and local men enthusiastically joined them in a game which began to re-discover its international nature. Mexicans, Chinese and Italians among many other nations began once more to play the dangerous and exciting game that had once taken the place of war. In 1904, a number of European associations asked England to help in organizing an international federation; it is, however, a curious fact that she refused to do so and let world football develop on its own for many years. It was only in the 1950s that England returned to the international scene.

Note   The division into two paragraphs is suggested by the two important sub-topics of

the text: 1 Alcock's work, and 2 the
internationalization of the game. It is not
essential.

g. Ireland/Irish (adj); Irishmen and
   Irishwomen (n)
h. Cyprus/Cypriot(s)
i. Tanzania/Tanzanian(s)
j. Japanese/Japanese (adj; n)

7.7 1 a. China/(a) Chinese
b. Uruguay/(a) Uruguayan
c. Indonesia/(an) Indonesian
d. Iraq/(an) Iraqi
e. Greece/(a) Greek
f. Morocco/(a) Moroccan
g. Nigeria/(a) Nigerian
h. Peru/(a) Peruvian
i. Switzerland/(a) Swiss
j. Turkey/Turkish; a Turk

2 a. Scotland/Scottish (adj); Scots (n)
b. France/French (adj); Frenchmen and
   Frenchwomen (n)
c. England/English (adj); Englishmen and
   Englishwomen (n)
d. the U.S.A./American(s)
e. Norway/Norwegian(s)
f. Iceland/Icelandic (adj); Icelanders (n)

3 a. a Welsh(wo)man d. a French(wo)man
b. a Dane   e. a Spaniard
c. an Argentinian f. a Belgian

4 a. Chinese
b. Greek
c. Burmese art
d. Cantonese dialect
e. Mexican customs
f. Irish history
g. Persian Empire
h. American museum
i. Spanish and Portuguese wine
j. East German, Polish and Hungarian
   materials

5 1e; 2c; 3g; 4i; 5a; 6h; 7b; 8j; 9f; 10d

7.8 Swimming as a Sport

p = a punctuation problem
g = a grammatical problem
s = a spelling problem

p As a sport, swimming can be very satisfying; you can, for
g example, swim indoors or outdoors, as one of a team, or
   alone. You can swim for physical fitness or for a challenge.
g You can swim to prove something or to win something or
   to get somewhere or simply because you like the water.   5

s   For some people swimming is a pleasant but not very active
g thing, to be enjoyed on a sunny day at the beach with a picnic
s afterwards. For others it is a highly competitive business, even
g a profession. It is a sport which/that demands hours of
   disciplined practice.   10

s p   Whether you become a once-a-year holiday swimmer or a
g famous international champion, you must have had a reason to
g start in the first place. Perhaps your mother and father were
s keen swimmers;[1] perhaps you had an enthusiastic teacher at
p g school; perhaps your friends got you interested. Like most   15
p people, however, you probably began at the shallow end of a

155

public swimming pool, and only after a lot of practice did
s   you get to the deep end, the diving board and finally the
sp   excitements of the open sea.

pg   Swimming, of course, is not the only watersport today. There   20
are many: sailing, canoeing, waterskiing, surfing, dinghies
s   and the like. There is also a great variety of kinds of
g   swimming: shallow water swimming, racing and diving on
the one hand, and deepsea swimming and diving with the aid
of flippers and aqualungs on the other hand. People who   25
enjoy these pastimes and professions do so because, like fish,
they feel at home in the water.

Feeling at home in the water means not only enjoyment of
s   water under good conditions, but also confidence and
courage under difficult conditions. There are dangers in the   30
water, whether or not it is the open sea. People can and do
p   drown, even capable swimmers who go beyond what they
g   can safely do. There are times when a good swimmer needs to
concentrate on saving his or her own life, or the life of
p   another person who is in danger of drowning. Under such   35
ps   conditions, it is vital not to panic and create unnecessary
problems for everybody. The rules for survival therefore
p   include keeping calm, being able to float for a long time and
s   the ability to tread water while waiting to be rescued.

¹ OR your mother or father was a keen swimmer; . . .

Notes

1 The semi-colon used in line 1 need not be used; a period is equally acceptable.

2 At various points throughout the text commas could be used differently. For example, someone who likes the firmness and clarity of parenthetical commas can put them round 'of course' (line 23 of the original text) and 'therefore' (line 43).

Additionally, those who like always to have commas after introductory phrases might wish to have them after 'For some people' (line 7), and 'For others' (line 9).

3 The inverted form 'did you' (lines 20–21) is not a grammatical mistake but a construction regularly employed after such introductory phrases as 'only after'.

7.9   Competitive Swimming

Interest in competitive swimming has increased at all levels in recent years. Individuals have competed for years against each other, but one very interesting new thing in world swimming as a sport is the growth of what is called 'age-group swimming'. This kind of competition began in the United States in the 1950s and has now spread to almost every country of/in the world. In each country there are national governing bodies that organize various forms of competitive swimming and other watersports. Competitions are arranged not only for/between/among adults but also for younger swimmers of the same age range. Events are usually arranged in two-year steps; for example, 12-year-old and 13-year-old youngsters compete as/in a group. Racing distances vary according to age group, and in some places such as Australia even very young competitors are given a chance to compete over fairly long distances up to 1,500 metres. Most swimming clubs now have age-group teams and arrange special training and practice sessions for them.

UNIT 8

8.1 a. F: It is about 4–5,000 years old.
    b. **T**
    c. **T**
    d. **F**: You go up and down hillsides as well as across flat lands, etc.
    e. **T**
    f. **T**
    g. **T**
    h. **F**: Women do as well as, if not often better than, men.
    i **T**
    j **F**: There are three kinds of skiers, including the two mentioned and the third kind who use skis as an everyday wintertime necessity.

8.2 a. According; Dictionary; strapped
    b. Northern; Europeans; their; business
    c. skiing; developed
    d. excellent
    e. prefers; skiing; normally
    f. barriers; competent; muscular
    g. mountainsides; bicycles
    h. practice; knowledge
    i varies; percent; purchase
    j preferably; advantage; equipment; properly

8.3 Nil

8.4 1i; 2f; 3g; 4j; 5c; 6h; 7d; 8e; 9a; 10b

8.5 Number work: First Stage Nil
Number Work: Second Stage

    a. fifteen-foot wall **or** 15-foot wall
    b. forty-foot boat **or** 40-foot boat
    c. ten-ton truck **or** 10-ton truck
    d. 12,000-ton tanker

    e. 45-year plan
    f. ten-year project **or** 10-year project
    g. thirteen-year-old boy **or more commonly** 13-year-old boy
    h. 35-year-old bank manager
    i. eight-week-old baby **or** 8-week-old baby
    j. 17-year-old dispute
    k. 70-million-year-old fossil
    l. 1949 engine
    m. 1977 model
    n. 1982 design
    o. 1974 edition
    p. 1972 Club
    q. 15th-century house
    r. seventh-century manuscript **or** 7th-century manuscript
    s. 14th-century castle
    t. fourth-year student **or** 4th-year students
    u. a 50-year-old factory manager lives in an 18th-century house
    v. 50-foot(-long) 1980 boat

8.6 Numbers in a Text (treated as a single paragraph)

When the *Oxford English Dictionary* (also known as the *New English Dictionary* and 'Murray's Dictionary') was first published in 1928, it was already 71 years old. Its story actually began in the year 1857, when a learned clergyman, Richard Chenevix Trench, spoke to the Philological Society in England about various deficiencies in the dictionaries of the time. The Society OR society decided not long afterwards to create an entirely new kind of dictionary that would provide the life-histories of as many English words as possible, but its members hardly appreciated that the task would take so long and that, by 1928, their employees would have collected and defined no less than 414,825 words. The Dictionary OR dictionary had a succession of eminent editors (four Englishmen: Herbert Coleridge, Frederick Furnivall, Henry Bradley and C.T. Onions; and two Scotsmen: James Murray and William Craigie). Volunteers from all over the world helped in the enterprise and worked unbelievably hard on it. A Mr Austin is said to have sent in 165,000 quotations, a Mr Douglas 136,000, and a Dr Helwich of Vienna some 50,000. In 1879, when Murray succeeded Furnivall in leading the project, he took over from him 1¾ tons of material – and that was only halfway between the birth and the completion of the work.

8.7 Variety in a Text

1 lines 1 and 2
2 lines 2 to 4
3 line 5
4 lines 4, 20, 37 and 52
5 line 10; lines 14 and 15; lines 23–24; line 36; line 40; line 45; line 51
6 line 2; lines 18–19; lines 34–35
7 lines 6 and 7; line 12
8 line 29
9 lines 22–23; line 25; lines 27–28; lines 41–42, lines 48–50
10 line 48

8.8
a. (**British**) One can always hire skiing equipment at the resort if one wants to. One can save quite a lot of money that way.

(**American**) One can always rent skiing equipment at the resort if he wants to. He can save quite a lot of money that way.

b. You should always try to read the quality of the snow and change your style accordingly.

c. (**British**) One might suppose that skiing is quite a modern activity, with a relatively short history. If one supposed that, one would be wrong.

(**American**) One might suppose.... If he supposed that, he would be wrong.

d. 'I meet all my friends at the ski-resort,' she said.

e. Whatever your preference ...

f. ... Well, if I must go, I must go,' said the king, unhappily.

(**Note** that, especially in the past, kings tended to use what we call 'the royal use of *we*'. In that case, His Majesty might have said: 'Well, if we must go, we must go.')

8.9

(1) a	(6) up	(11) of	
(2) so that	(7) out of	(12) that	
(3) can	(8) at	(13) so	
(4) your	(9) as	(14) is	
(5) when	(10) on	(15) down	

8.10 **Nil**

UNIT 9

9.1
1 a. **T**
   b. **F**: The Americans did not use this term; the British did.
   c. **F**: The thrill element is still significant.
   d. **T**
   e. **F**: India can be said to rival the United States.
   f. **T**
   g. **F**: The cinema has not done too well when faced with television.
   h. **T**
   i **F**: Hollywood co-operates with the TV companies.
   j **T**

2 a. two examples: line 3–4; line 40
   b. four examples: line 5; line 8; lines 25–26; line 57
   c. six examples: line 17; lines 22–23; line 36; line 50; line 53; line 58
   d. nine examples: line 3 (twice); line 16; line 24 (twice); line 56 (three times); line 60
   e. three examples: line 11; line 32; line 53
   f. seven examples: lines 1, 36, 42 (twice), 46 (the cinema); line 3 (the 'movie theatre'); line 3 (the 'picture house');

lines 39 & 41–42 (the live theatre);
line 48 (the public movie); line 49 (the
private tube); line 54–55 (the videotape
industry)

g. nine examples: lines 13 & 14 (using
that); lines 27 & 28 (*that*); lines 29 & 31
(*that*); lines 31 & 32 (*which*); lines 34
& 35 (*whose*); lines 44 & 45 (*in
which*); lines 48 & 49 (*that*); lines 55
& 56 (*whom*); lines 58 & 59 (*that*)
(**Note** Other clauses beginning with
that (lines 46, 47, & 53) are not
relative clauses but noun clauses, that
is, clauses with the same function as a
noun.)

h. lines 19 to 24; lines 24 to 28

i. any ten of the following: movie theatre,
picture house, cinema halls,
Hollywood, film capital, United States,
music-hall entertainment, thrill
element, science-fiction extravaganza,
story-related, story film, Train
Robbery, film-makers, First World
War, New World, Great War, home
and export business, video games,
dinosaur ancestor, miniature cinema,
TV wall screens, living rooms, TV
companies, videotape industry,
celluloid dreams (**Note** Convincing
arguments can also be made for 'silent
films' and 'special effects', as adjective
compounds like *blackboard*; and for
'technicolor', 'television', and
'photography' as technical compounds.
'TV' can also be considered as an
abbreviated form of a compound.)

j. the beginning of the fourth paragraph
(line 29)

9.2 Nil

9.3   1 E,C,A,F,H,G,D,B
2 C,E,A,G,B,I,F,H,D

The expedition was made up of both men
and women. One of the women, a nurse,
said:

'At times it was frightening on the rapids,
but it was exciting to know you were the first
people to go over them.'

She was asked by a journalist how the men
had felt about having women with them on
the trip.

'I think they were a bit annoyed at first,'
she answered, 'but later they accepted us.'

That was probably all to the good,
because the journey took four months and
covered 2,700 miles.

9.5

(1) b,c,a	(8) a,c,b	(15) b,a,c
(2) b,c,a	(9) c,a,b	(16) a,b,c
(3) c,a,b	(10) c,b,a	(17) a,b,c
(4) a,b,c	(11) a,c,b	(18) c,a,b
(5) c,a,b	(12) c,a,b	(19) a,b,c
(6) b,c,a	(13) b,c,a	(20) b,a,c
(7) b,a,c	(14) c,b,a	

9.6   a. motherly
b. noisy
c. unfriendly
d. insane
e. incapable
f. carelessly
g. independently
h. receiver
i. noiseless, cat-like/catlike
j. **British** skilfully **American** skillfully
k. stony, unromantic
l. shirtless, sunny
m. useful, scientific
n. angry, perfectly, harmless
o. impossibility, carefully, insufficient
p. untrained, flawless, microscopically,
unfortunate, imperfections
q. unprofessional, impractical,
unintelligent, totally, unlikely
r. powerful, political, national,
mathematical, technical
s. Normally, confidence, athletic,
incredibly, unsure, justice
t. unemotionally, psychological, practical,
exceptionally, impersonally

9.7 Nil